MOTIVATION.
ACTION.
RESULTS.

How Network Marketing Leaders Move Their Teams

KEITH & TOM "BIG AL" SCHREITER

Motivation. Action. Results.

Published by Fortune Network Publishing
PO Box 890084
Houston, TX 77289 USA
Telephone: +1 (281) 280-9800

ISBN: 1-892366-64-9
ISBN-13: 978-1-892366-64-1

CONTENTS

PREFACE

Is motivation an art? Or is it a science?

Maybe a bit of both. The mind is the least-understood part of humans, but it does leave clues. We can work with these clues to further motivate ourselves, and others.

This book is not a reference or textbook on the science of human motivation.

So what is this book?

It's a collection of practical motivation techniques that we can use in our network marketing business.

Motivating our new distributors isn't our only task as leaders in network marketing. However, it is certainly an important task.

Let's have fun discovering some of the interesting ways we can motivate ourselves, and others, to higher achievement.

—Keith Schreiter and Tom "Big Al" Schreiter

DONUTS.

Temporary, external motivation:

1. I am hungry. (Motivated)

2. I eat a dozen donuts. (Happy)

3. I am full. (Un-motivated)

Permanent, internal motivation:

1. I am hungry. (Motivated)

2. I eat a dozen donuts. (Happy)

3. I am still hungry. (Strong internal motivation)

Yes, both ways of motivation work. However, permanent motivation should be our eventual goal. We will discuss both types of motivation in this book.

MOTIVATING THE UNMOTIVATED DISTRIBUTOR.

Unmotivated distributors?

It could happen.

This is never mentioned in the opportunity meetings, but sometimes distributors become inactive or even ... quit!

They don't participate in the duplication process. They are messing up our plan.

What is our job as network marketing leaders?

Our job is to motivate and lead, right?

If motivation is one of our main duties, wouldn't it be nice if we had many different ways to accomplish it?

What if a friend asked us, "What do you do for a living?"

Suppose we answered, "I am a network marketing leader. One of my primary duties is to motivate my organization. I don't have a clue how to do it."

Aaaack! I am sure our friend would have a great laugh and think, "What an idiot!"

Motivation is huge.

There isn't just one way to motivate others. There are many ways.

All types of motivation have good points and bad points, and some types will only work in limited circumstances.

Let's get down to business and establish some of the ways we can motivate people.

THE DOWNSIDE TO REWARD MOTIVATION.

We call Sam, our semi-alive distributor, and say, "Did you know that if you sold just $6,000 more in products, you qualify for the company's new car bonus?"

Wow! That should get Sam's adrenaline going.

But, it **doesn't**.

Sam thinks, "I wish my sponsor would stop calling me. There is no way that I could sell even $50 of our products. Besides, I just got 150 new cable channels and I have my own problems to think about. Heck, I am already getting carpal tunnel syndrome from pressing buttons on my new high-speed remote control. I might become handicapped! Anyway, my 1972 Ford Pinto still runs just fine as long as the rust build-up prevents the gas tank from leaking. I don't need a new car now. I don't have time to go out and get rejected. Ooooh. My wrist and thumb are hurting more. Just let me channel-surf to the Hypochondriac Channel. Maybe I should turn my phone off ..."

That's the trouble with reward motivation. Sometimes it **doesn't** work.

Why? There are several reasons.

Sam doesn't believe he can do it. He hasn't sold $6,000 of products in the past. That is proof enough that it can't be done. The fact that the network marketing company has a car bonus plan doesn't change Sam's beliefs or skills. He is still under-confident ... and more than a bit lazy.

Sam will take the path of **least resistance**. His car still runs. It is easier to patch his car than to get $6,000 in product sales. That would be a lot of work and rejection. It is easier to cut back on his car trips.

This is the old "donkey, carrot and the stick" story all over again. If you are not familiar with the story, it goes something like this:

If you want to make a stubborn donkey walk, put a carrot on the end of a stick and hold it in front of the donkey. If the donkey is hungry, the donkey will walk forward trying to bite the carrot. Works great ... **unless the donkey isn't hungry!** A "no appetite" donkey will ignore your carrot reward and just stand there, unmotivated.

Sounds pretty familiar, doesn't it? If a distributor needs more money for a larger home, the distributor has two choices:

Choice #1: Go to work. Sponsor new people. Retail. Get rejected. Drive to meetings. Study hard and learn more skills. Put up with disappointment. Attend training seminars. Make phone calls and take the risk that all this effort might not pay off.

Choice #2: Stay home. Learn to exist in cramped living conditions. Enjoy that new cable television system.

Which choice will most people make?

Choice #2.

Choice #2 is easier. There is no risk. It is the path of least resistance. Existing in cramped living conditions is like the donkey ... it feels better to just stand still than to reach out for that carrot.

This is why 98% of distributors won't try when our network marketing company runs a contest. They find it easier to be content and to just stay where they are.

If reward motivation really worked, everyone in our network marketing company would be at the top position, collecting the top bonus percentage, riding around in the top bonus car available, and enjoying every vacation incentive.

Rewards can work, but only if people are hungry. Most people aren't hungry. They get along in life just fine at their present level of income and comfort.

Rewards are like bribes. The message we convey is:

"We will give you this, if you do that."

That means people have a choice. Unfortunately, people tend to pick the easier, safer choice.

Reward motivation has limits. We need to have additional ways to motivate our downlines.

However, just because reward motivation isn't perfect doesn't mean we should never use it. If we choose to use reward motivation, we want to make it the best that we can.

Let's look at some reward motivation ideas that do work. And yes, this is temporary motivation, but we have to start somewhere.

REWARD MOTIVATION EXAMPLES THAT WORK.

Rewards! Stuff! Prizes! That sounds pretty good.

The basic motivation summary is, "We will give you this, if you do that."

Let's look at the positive side. Here are some examples of reward motivations that have worked in the past.

Win a trip to Hawaii!

Years ago, a network marketing company sold water filters. Their distributors were not trained salespeople. The company's marketing plan was to have the distributor loan the water filter to a prospect. This allowed the prospect to use the water filter for one week. Then, hopefully the prospect would sell himself on the advantages of keeping the water filter.

Even though the distributors were "loaning" the water filters, many people were reluctant to take them. They were afraid of a big sales pitch when the salesman would return to pick up the water filter after one week.

The company's marketing department devised a plan to make it easier to loan out the water filters. Every prospect who used a water filter for a week would get a chance to win a trip to Hawaii. Every week the company would choose a winner.

So now, all the distributor had to say was, "Please try the water filter for one week. The worst that can happen is that you get a free chance to win a trip to Hawaii. The best that can happen is that your water tastes wonderful and you will want to keep the water filter."

This reward made it easy to loan out water filters. In this case, reward motivation worked quite well.

But, it gets better.

The company also tapped into another method of motivation. Here is what they added.

The company taught each distributor to say, "You will get a free entry into the drawing for the Hawaii holiday this week. And, if you win the holiday, they will give me a free holiday also. So please take the water filter for one week. Not only can you win a free Hawaiian holiday, but if you win, I can get a free holiday also."

Now, the prospect felt guilty if they did not take the water filter for one week. **Guilt motivation** works too. It was hard for prospects to refuse to take the water filter. They didn't want to be responsible for the distributor not having a chance to win a trip to Hawaii.

Lottery ticket rewards.

This is a great way to prospect for new distributors, and keep your current downline active, week after week after week. The cost? About one dollar, the price of a lottery ticket.

Many prospects have huge disappointments in their lives. Sometimes they feel like giving up. Their solution? Buy some lottery tickets. Temporary hope is better than no hope at all.

Now, if buying lottery tickets is their final act of desperation, then that is sad. These prospects need something that will offer a better chance of success. Maybe something such as ... network marketing!

Say to the prospect, "I have a better plan than lottery tickets. You will have a much better chance at winning.

"Join my network marketing program. Do what I do (recommend and promote our products and opportunity), and don't stop until you become rich. Each week I will buy a lottery ticket for us and split the winnings with you. We'll do this every week. We will be on our way to becoming rich in our network marketing business. And, each week we will have a chance of winning the lottery!"

What a great way to give a bit of hope to someone who is feeling down. What a great way to sponsor new people. What a great way to keep people working on their business, week after week after week.

Now, it doesn't take much imagination to realize our new distributors could extend this offer to their prospects and downline also. That's leverage.

Oh, but it gets better. The "fear of loss" motivation works with this lottery ticket technique.

The semi-discouraged distributor wants to participate. Why? Because if the distributor doesn't participate that week, and that week's lottery ticket actually does win, oh my! The distributor would feel that he lost out on half the winnings because he didn't work on his business that week.

Don't let this idea pass you by.

Think about other ways we can use a simple lottery ticket to motivate your current group.

We could buy a lottery ticket for each of the new distributors who attend your fast-start training. Or, offer to buy them a lottery ticket every week for 10 weeks, if they just accomplish a certain goal.

Or how about handing out free lottery tickets at the opportunity meeting to distributors and guests?

Wow! Wow! Wow!

This works for your products too!

In our book, *51 Ways and Places to Sponsor New Distributors*, we explained how using a losing lottery ticket could motivate more people to become customers.

Here is the excerpt:

For example, let's say you sold diet products and couldn't afford advertising. Maybe all you could afford for your promotion was one month's worth of diet products.

So what could you do? How about a contest for LOSERS?

Announce that anyone can enter your contest, but they must have two qualifications.

1. They must own a losing lottery ticket.

2. They must want to lose weight.

Hold a drawing of the submitted losing lottery tickets and give away a one-month's supply of diet products to the winner.

You would get plenty of word-of-mouth advertising and publicity from such an innovative campaign. Make the campaign more interesting by holding the drawing at the local donut shop or pizzeria.

* If you sold skin care, how about a "lose those wrinkles" contest?

* If you sold travel services, how about a "lose those winter blues" contest for people who hate winter?

* If you wanted to promote your business opportunity, how about a "lose your boss" contest?

* Or maybe a contest to see who could submit the best reason for "losing their alarm clock." Wow. They would be ultra-qualified prospects.

How about some more short-term reward ideas?

A free five-week leadership course, including dinner!

Every Thursday night from 7:00 p.m. to 10:00 p.m. we hold a dinner training meeting at a local restaurant. We conduct this training meeting for five consecutive Thursday nights.

How much does this cost?

Imagine that dinner for our new distributor costs $20. Our meeting room is free since the restaurant will provide a separate room for our "dinner training" and guests.

If we paid for our new distributor's leadership training and dinner, our total cost is only $100 over five weeks per distributor.

Now, what did we buy for our $100 investment?

First, we bought a new distributor. This unique five-week training program, complete with dinner, was the spectacular incentive that motivated our prospect to join.

Second, we bought guaranteed attendance at our next five training meetings. Free food will always draw a crowd.

Third, we bought a trained distributor who may develop into a potential leader. Just think of how much information, belief and motivation we can transfer during these five training sessions.

Can we afford to buy distributors for $100?

If we can, we could buy them by the truckload. If we can't, we'll change the promotion to something less expensive.

Maybe we could set a small requirement, that the new distributor must make a sale that week, or that the new distributor sponsors someone new. Or maybe the distributor could pay for the meal so our total cost is zero. Just remember, the more we invest into our new distributors, the more likely they'll attend.

But usually a well-trained new distributor can produce enough volume, and sponsor enough people, to make this a great return on our $100 promotional investment.

Get others to help us with our reward motivation contests.

We can engage the spouse to provide consistent day-to-day motivation for our distributor.

How?

In the 1950s, one company had a contest for the salesmen to find new accounts. All of the salesmen were men.

The grand prize for opening 20 new accounts was a full-length mink coat for the spouse (probably politically incorrect now.) Since this was quite a luxury in the 1950s, most of the wives were very excited. They provided plenty of motivation for their husbands to accept the rejection that comes with prospecting for new accounts.

But the company was taking no chances. Each week the company mailed a postcard to the salesman's home with the number of new accounts opened so far. Of course the wife saw the postcard first. She knew that if she wanted the mink coat, she had to continue motivating and inspiring her husband.

The company got help. The company used weekly postcards to engage the wife to help them motivate the salesman.

There is a lesson here.

We don't have to motivate the distributor. Instead, maybe we can engage the distributor's spouse, children, co-workers or friends to help us inspire the distributor to greater heights.

And just so you don't think this is sexist ... here is how a company with a female sales force could motivate the husbands to inspire their wives.

Offer the latest game console as the grand prize. Most videogame-addicted husbands would chauffeur their wives to each appointment. And football tickets to the big game? Oh yes, many husbands would be the biggest cheerleaders for their wife's success.

Even your distributor's boss can help with motivation.

Don't forget, our distributor has a boss at the day job. The negative, overbearing boss will provide plenty of reasons **daily** to motivate our distributor to work hard to leave that dream-sucking job.

In the search for profits, many companies require their employees to work harder, to work longer, and even have reduced benefits. Employees notice this. All we have to do is remind our distributor of his day job.

Yes, frustration can be a strong motivator.

Other reward contest ideas.

What's hot? Well, cash is boring and cars are an old idea. What can we do that is different?

Idea #1: Win our contest and we will pay your income taxes for a whole year! People hate paying taxes and would love getting all their tax money back in their pocket.

Idea #2: Win our contest and we will make your mortgage payment this month! Or if it was a big contest, we could make their mortgage payment for one year! A mortgage payment is usually the biggest bill in a family's budget. I can see the spouse getting excited about having all that extra money to spend that month.

How about a cruise?

Currently, Caribbean cruises are cheap, only about $100-$150 a day per person. So a seven-day cruise would only be $700-$1,000 or sometimes even less. That includes meals, entertainment, the stateroom ... and plenty of sun and fun.

Many people dream about the day they can afford to take a Caribbean cruise. They just can't seem to budget for the cruise. We can help them with this incentive.

Start the incentive one year in advance. That means the cruise would only cost as little as $60 a month for the next twelve months.

Ask yourself, "What could my distributor do that would earn me an extra $60 a month?"

Now, this could be a lot of things, but for purposes of demonstration, let's imagine this. If a distributor in our downline sponsored two new people that month, we would earn an extra $60.

That is achievable. Anyone can sponsor two people in a month if they really want to. So this incentive appeals to everyone.

Here is what we can announce as our personal group cruise contest.

The "My Team" Group Cruise.

Come join everyone on "My Team" for a seven-day Caribbean cruise. This luxury cruise includes all meals and buffets, entertainment, your cabin and more. Join the team, meet new people, explore the different islands, and keep the memories forever.

The cruise is only $700 and you can make 12 payments of only $60 a month. But it gets better!

Would you like me to make your payments for you? If you sponsor two new distributors in a month, I will make that month's payment for you! Do this each month, and I will pay for your entire cruise! Join us on this cruise, and please, let me make all or most of those monthly payments for you!

Here is the magic.
Twelve reasons to get excited.

First, everyone gets excited about a free cruise. They love it when someone else pays.

Second, the contest isn't one of those where only the top ten distributors win and everyone else loses. Everyone feels they have a chance.

Third, if they don't qualify for one month or two months, they don't lose everything. They can just make those payments themselves.

Fourth, if they qualify for ten months, they are happy to make the other two payments themselves. An inexpensive vacation!

Fifth, new people that join part-way through the incentive period can still qualify for some of their payments to be free.

Sixth, many people will pay for their spouse to come also. If we wanted, we could expand the cruise incentive to say they could qualify for two payments if they sponsored four people that month.

Seventh, a lot of people who qualify won't come. They may have other obligations, conflicts, or maybe they don't like cruising. This gives us extra money to spend on those who do come.

Eighth, everyone pays for their own transportation to get to the cruise port. You don't have to fund that. People use air miles from friends or drive as a group. They find a way.

Ninth, bonding. Our team bonds by living together every day on the cruise ship. It is not like a hotel or resort where people go their own ways. On a cruise they eat together, go to shows together, party together, do land tours together ... they are bonding the whole time. This really creates loyalty and team spirit.

Tenth, memories. Life is measured by the number of memories, not by the number of years. Our distributors will talk about this cruise for a long time.

Eleventh, recruiting. More sponsoring happens with this incentive. This is consistent sponsoring, not just a one-time burst. This is a great incentive for new people to join. The upcoming cruise gives our team something extra to talk about.

Twelfth, the new team members we build with this incentive pay us back month after month, and year after year.

Can you see a cruise in your future?

How to make your contest investment go a lot further.

We don't like to waste money. If we invest in a contest or promotion for our group, we want to get the maximum results for our dollars. Let's look at how to keep everyone involved by eliminating "unfair" competition.

Who is the real competition?

We want our distributors to compete against themselves, not against each other. This way we can get more distributors to take part in the competition.

What if we only have one big prize to give away, a trip to Hawaii? The distributor who sponsors the most new distributors for the next 30 days will win the prize. Here is what most of the distributors in our organization will think:

"Oh, John Superstar will win the contest. He always sponsors more people than we do. He has lots of prospects he can talk to over the next 30 days. Since there is no way I can beat John Superstar, I won't even bother to try. I will sit at home, watch television and eat more ice cream."

When we force our distributors to compete against each other, most distributors won't participate. They feel like they don't have a chance. Instead, consider having our distributors compete against themselves.

For example, imagine having a contest where any distributor who sponsors a new person in the next 30 days wins a special seat at your monthly leadership banquet. This means everyone can compete – and everyone can win.

More distributors will try to sponsor new people because they feel they can win.

In my book, *26 Instant Marketing Ideas To Build Your Network Marketing Business*, I wrote about this successful campaign:

The monthly banquet.

Each month our group had a dinner at a famous Chinese restaurant. The only way you could come to this special dinner was by invitation. You would pay for your dinner, but you had to have a special invitation to attend.

How did you earn the invitation?

You simply sponsored one new distributor during the month. That's it. If you sponsored a new distributor, you received an invitation. The real value to the distributor was being part of a special group for the monthly dinner.

To make things even better, the new distributor (or distributors) you sponsored received an invitation also.

Picture this. Can you see yourself with a room full of active, sponsoring distributors and the new distributors they sponsored? It's exciting!

What was the cost?

About $15 per person. I negotiated a special group price for the dinner on a Monday. It was a day when the local Chinese restaurant had very little business.

I asked, "How much for an evening buffet meal?" The owner said, "$19.95 plus your drink."

However, I had a lot more to offer. I asked what the price would be if I could get 40 people there at one time. The restaurant owner said, "Only $15, and that includes the drink."

Sold! If you can get a deal like this, the restaurant owner is happy. He is going to make some money on Monday night and keep some employees happy with the extra business. Plus, the restaurant owner knows his food is so good, that our group will certainly tell others. He is looking forward to some high-profit referral business.

Because we have to eat somewhere, the restaurant puts your group in a private room. Your banquet can now include a bit of a training session ... and you don't have the expense of renting a meeting room. If the restaurant owner doesn't immediately offer a private room, say, "Sometimes we have a little toast or a speech, and we don't want to bother your other customers. Do you have a little banquet or meeting room where we could eat so that we don't disturb anyone?"

During our "banquet," we had trophies for the top recruiters, the top retailers, special prizes for other categories and a great group spirit. Not bad for an inexpensive contest where everyone paid for their own meals.

Even though each distributor was competing against himself to qualify, there was also group pressure to make sure you never missed the monthly dinner. You wanted your friends and downline to see you there every month.

Imagine this scenario. Mrs. Distributor purchases a new dress for this month's banquet. She can't wait to see her regular friends and to catch up on all the news since the last banquet.

It is now the 29th of the month. Her husband, Mr. Distributor, arrives home from work. Excited, Mrs. Distributor shows him the dress she just purchased for the monthly banquet. Since the banquet is only two days away, she asks, "And by the way, how many new distributors did you sponsor so far this month?"

He answers, "None."

Don't you think Mr. Distributor is going to make sure he sponsors someone tomorrow before he returns home? I think so too.

Motivation can come from peers, spouses, and even competitors.

The bottom line?

This one simple dinner kept leaders and distributors active and sponsoring every month.

Improving our contests.

When offering a contest prize, we can improve our results by making sure that our prize:

1. Creates excitement. If our prize is practical, boring and dull, don't expect people to rush to qualify. A toaster or a vacuum cleaner will decrease motivation. But 100 lottery tickets or a first-class evening on the town will get our distributors excited.

2. Has a high perceived value. A trip to Las Vegas feels more valuable than the cash equivalent. Dinner with the company president feels more valuable than the $20 cost of dinner.

3. Has only a short time period, whenever possible. It's easier to get excited when the contest lasts only a few days or weeks. A year-long contest requires constant reminders and re-motivation.

Do we want to build more cooperation within our group?

Yes, we all want to belong to a group. We are social.

We can make our reward motivation extra-effective by adding peer pressure to overcome the **fear of rejection.**

Many times we go out of our comfort zone just to help others.

In our contests, let's try offering a **group prize.** This way each person in the group feels the need to contribute. No one wants to let the other group members down.

Try this contest.

If we have five distributors, offer to take them to an evening of dinner and entertainment, but **only** if each of them sponsors at least one person.

The strong members of the group will easily sponsor one or more people.

The weaker members of the group will go beyond their comfort zone and try to sponsor someone. They don't want to be **responsible** for the group not winning the contest.

Best of all, the stronger members of the group will try to help the weaker members get their new recruits.

Everyone wins.

Now we have doubled our group size from five distributors to 10 distributors at a very low cost.

Add this to the contest. If one person sponsors five new distributors, then everyone in the drawing automatically wins.

They will all be cheering for that one superstar to sponsor five new distributors.

This will reduce jealousy and increase a spirit of cooperation. They will help each other in the hope that everyone wins.

As a bonus, our distributors will collaborate and plot how to beat the system so that everyone will win. That means we win too!

Prizes and contests do work, so have fun creating your own incentives.

FEAR MOTIVATION.

A child is 20 inches (50 cm) tall. He looks up to his dad, who is 6 feet (182 cm) tall in comparison. The dad says to the child,

"Sit!"

What does the child think?

"Yeah, okay, not a bad idea, maybe I should sit. Especially since Dad seems to be in a bad mood! I think I will sit down ... right here!"

Now, that is effective! Years later, when the child is 18 years old, his dad looks up to his six-foot-six-inch tall, 240 lb. son and says,

"Sit!"

Do you think the father's message still carries the same threatening tone? Or do you think Dad's demand has lost something over the years? It is just not quite the same as when the child was small.

So, maybe fear **isn't** such a good motivator when people have other options.

Some people experience fear motivation on their jobs. The boss may say,

"If you don't do what I tell you to do, you are fired!"

Think about this. How would you feel if someone were to use fear motivation on you?

Would you feel de-motivated? Angry? Resentful? Or, perhaps you would develop the "I will get even with the boss" attitude.

Do you believe that there is a place in network marketing for this type of thinking? No. We shouldn't threaten our downline.

Network marketing distributors are **volunteers**, so we don't have the leverage that fear motivation needs.

Let's say that you phone someone in your downline and say,

"If you don't sponsor someone today, you are fired! And, I will never call you again!"

Your distributor would likely think,

"Never call me again? Hey, is that a promise? All right! I won't have to hear from my jerk sponsor again."

Fear is one of our least-effective motivators. However, for **some** situations, it works well.

Fear of failure = embarrassment.

When we start our business, many of our friends and relatives tell us, "Oh, that won't work. You will never be successful. You were stupid to try."

To go back to our friends and admit that they were right, ugh! That scene is hard to stomach.

One of our primary fear motivators is to "avoid being wrong." That means we will work harder, plow through obstacles, and have more persistence. Why? To avoid the disgrace of returning to our naysayers and admitting they were right.

You could casually say this from time to time, within hearing distance of your downline:

"We can quit at any time. Then, we'll go back to our negative friends and relatives and have them say, 'We told you so! We said you were stupid to try to make your life better.'"

Ouch.

Or, we can continue through some temporary obstacles. Then we can tell our negative friends and relatives, "I told you so! I told you I could make my life better if I tried."

This little scene in our mind can motivate us through some tough challenges.

I don't want to be left behind!

Imagine you are three years old. Your mother takes you to the market. You are bored. You begin to wander. You go to explore, and your mother quickly pulls you back. You want to see something interesting, but again your mother runs after you and pulls you back.

After some time, your mother says, "Hang on to my dress! If you run away one more time, I will leave this market, and you will be left behind!"

You are only three years old. Your mother is your sole source of survival. You panic. You grab your mother's dress with your hand, and are afraid to let go. If your mother leaves without you, you won't survive.

The fear of being left behind works everywhere in your life.

Later in school, your teacher knows you have this "I don't want to be left behind" program in your mind. She pulls you aside and says, "If you don't do your homework, your classmates will graduate to the next grade, and you will be left behind."

Suddenly, we are motivated to do our homework. We don't want to be left behind when our classmates move on to the next grade.

This program gets reinforced in high school. All the cool kids are invited to a party, but not us. We were ... left behind. That bad feeling feeds the "left behind" program in our minds.

This is why we panic when we are late for an airplane flight. The program in our mind is, "I don't want to be left behind."

You can activate this program in yourself and others through many different means.

For example, there will be recognition at your next big meeting. You could say, "Most distributors who join this month will be recognized for achieving the first rank in our plan. Make sure that you qualify. When everyone goes onstage to receive their awards, you don't want to be left behind. You don't want to be the only one sitting in the audience clapping."

Or you could say this: "The convention is our most important event of the year. Make sure to get your convention ticket now. You don't want to be left behind. You don't want to be at home wondering why you never get a bonus check, while others are at the convention learning new ways to make their bonus checks grow."

Or you could say this: "Qualifying for this year's cruise incentive is going to be easy. Make sure you qualify early. You want to be on the cruise ship sending postcards to your friends. You don't want to be the person staying at home, getting postcards from their friends."

Fear does motivate.

Fear of failure, fear of embarrassment, and fear of being left behind. All are great motivators when facing tough obstacles.

But how about another example?

When to use competition within your group.

Red personalities love competition. The prize is meaningless. The honor and recognition of winning is everything.

For example, consider the old "Steak and Beans" contest. At the beginning of the week, two distributors agree to the following:

"Whoever sells the most product by Friday night gets to eat a steak dinner. The loser gets to eat beans. Plus, the loser must pay for both dinners and watch the victorious distributor enjoy his steak."

Watch how hard these ultra-competitive distributors will work just to win this contest. The best part is that the loser usually desires a rematch next week to restore his or her honor. That means more volume. All this productive effort occurs just for honor and recognition.

The best part is that this contest costs nothing, yet produces high results.

We don't have to limit this contest to just two distributors. Why not consider teams?

Now we have the extra motivation of distributors working harder to make sure they don't let their other team members down.

Many times the fear of losing is far greater than the motivation to win. That's just human nature.

The "Steak and Beans" contest uses recognition motivation and fear motivation. Both work. And both work well when used together.

Fear motivation could be as easy as this.

Bob Conklin told the story of a young boy who would forget to tuck his shirt tail into his pants. No matter how much his mother would complain, the young boy continued to run around with his shirt tail out.

His mother solved the problem with one simple little task. One day while sewing, she decided to sew some lady's white frilly lace onto her son's shirt tail.

Now her son was motivated to never allow his shirt tail to flop out of his pants again. Why? Fear of embarrassment.

Want another example of a simple solution for long-term motivation? This solution was just a "sound bite."

Zig Ziglar told the story of a young child who didn't want to brush his teeth. His mother solved the motivation problem by telling her son, "Just brush the teeth you want to keep."

Done.

OVERCOMING THE FEAR TO JOIN.

Risk. We hate risk.

For many prospects and distributors, the removal of risk opens the door to motivation.

Here is an example. We give our best presentation. Powerful benefits. Motivating examples and stories. And when we have finished our masterpiece, our prospect looks at us with ... **a blank stare.**

Our prospect just doesn't "get it." He doesn't see the big picture. He doesn't have a clue.

What is wrong? Our company is great. Our products are fantastic. The compensation plan can give our prospect financial freedom. So what's missing?

We forgot to consider that our prospects look at our opportunity from a completely different viewpoint. What is that different viewpoint?

<u>Their</u> viewpoint!

They look at things from where they are. Our prospects didn't experience the same motivational trainings and opportunity meetings we did. They will think small. Really small.

Here is an example to show how we think and see things differently.

(You are an educated, highly-motivated, super-intelligent reader of this book. We are psychic. We can tell these things.)

You bought this book because you experienced a deep desire to improve your networking business. You want to motivate others. And you want growth now.

However, guess what? There are some people in network marketing who haven't purchased this book. Isn't that amazing? Hard to believe, isn't it?

Anyway, let's look at why some people didn't buy this book.

Because they didn't put aside a few extra dollars in their bank accounts.

These are the people who need this book the most, aren't they? Look at it this way. What if someone worked for ten years and was not able to save a few dollars from his paycheck? Would we consider what they are doing a success or a failure?

Our thinking might be, "If ten years of hard work nets a person less than a few dollars, it is time to change his current plan."

Why would that person want to continue on the same path? In another ten years, this person will have the exact same result ... nothing. And to make matters worse, that person will be ten years older.

If our hand hurts because every day for ten years we slam the door on our hand, that is a clue. If we keep doing the same thing, slamming the door on our hand for the next ten years, nothing is going to change. We will continue to have an extremely sore hand.

If we want a different result, we have to change what we are doing.

What about the people who haven't been able to save a few dollars in their bank accounts with their entire life's efforts? Don't we think it is time they change what they are doing? Wouldn't it occur to them to say:

"Hey, I have been making the same decisions all my life, and look where it got me so far. Maybe I should get a little outside advice."

This is easy for us to see from the outside. It is harder to see if we are the person failing miserably. Sometimes when we are so deep into our world, we can't see to the end of our shirt sleeve.

This group of people needs new information, new techniques, new ways of doing their business, and a new plan for life. The problem is:

We can't see that when we don't have a few dollars.

This is the problem for our prospect at your opportunity meeting.

This is why he can't join. His attitude and vision are only about two inches long. The "few dollars" thinking is running his internal programs. Here is what goes through his mind:

"Yeah, it is a great business opportunity for someone who can do it. There is no way I can do it. Heck, I can barely keep my head above water now. My credit cards are over the limit. I am two car payments behind. My spouse says that I don't have a clue about anything.

"Everything I have done so far has gotten me to this point in my life: **broke.** If I join this opportunity, I will just pay a bunch of money for a kit and training. I won't earn anything and then I will **lose** all that money and then ... oh, heck. Let's just forget the whole thing. It is one of those deals that will work for a few special people. But I will just lose money again."

We can help.

We want to motivate our prospect to take a step forward. But to do this, we have to slow down, grab our prospect's hand, give him some confidence and say:

"Hey, listen, it is not such a big step. I will be walking right by your side. We can grow and learn on our way to our success. I am having success with this opportunity already. I don't intend to lose money. So if you'll walk beside me, we will do it together, okay?"

Will this approach work?

Will this be enough motivation to get your prospect to take that crucial first step?

Probably not.

It might work for some prospects. But most prospects have a lifetime of programming that keeps them exactly where they are. They want to be somewhere else. They know they have to do something different to get there. However, it is going to require a huge effort to take that crucial first step.

If we sincerely want to help this person (and that's a personal decision), we will have to make an extraordinary effort to break through that inertia.

Is it worth the effort?

Some people say,

"Only work with prospects who are ready to work."

This works fine when dealing with strangers. But, what if the prospect is your best friend? Your mother? The minister of your church? The brave person who saved you from a burning building?

We would think differently about these prospects. We would definitely put more time and effort into helping them become successful in our business. After all, there is more to our networking business than just the cold, hard numbers on our bonus check, right? There is a thing called "helping people."

So, what can we do to motivate and help this attitude-impaired and confidence-impaired individual? How can we make it easier for this person to take that first step?

Remember, we can't look at things from our perspective.

We are network marketing believers already.

We have to have empathy. We must look at this problem through the squinted, skeptical eyes of a prospect that has worked all his life and can't even show a few dollars for his efforts.

If we want to get through to this prospect, we must remove **all** the risk in his decision.

Our prospect's confidence level is so low that he is afraid to make any decision. Why? Because he is afraid to make a wrong decision.

His life is paralyzed. His life is all about avoiding a bad or foolish decision that will embarrass him in front of his friends and family.

If we take away the risk, it will be easier for our prospect to at least give our opportunity a try. If there is no risk, there is no chance to make a bad decision.

How can we remove the risk in our new prospect's network marketing business?

Consider our company's money-back guarantee.

Many times we just mention that our prospect can get his money back in 30 days or 60 days. But what does our prospect really think? This is what goes through his mind:

"Yeah, they say they will give my money back, but only if the kit is in good condition. I bet they say none of the 'used' kits are in good condition. The company will ignore my refund request. My sponsor won't return my calls or honor the guarantee. I bet I will have to get signed affidavits of my best efforts. Or maybe I will have to submit blood samples. I just know there is some fine print somewhere that I won't get my money back. This is too risky."

Here is one way we can overcome this skeptical thinking. We could say:

"Joe, there is no guarantee in life, but there is a guarantee if you try our opportunity. We want you to try our business for 60 days, with no risk to you.

"Here is what we do. At the end of 60 days, you will have a pretty good idea if this business is for you or not. Hey, maybe you'll have just won the lottery and you are not interested in working a part-time business anymore. If you win a million dollars in next month's lottery, trust me, we will understand.

"Anyway, at the end of 60 days, you and I sit down. If you don't want to continue with our business for any reason, that is okay. We only want you to continue if you feel that this business is for you. We want you to be committed to building your own empire, okay?

"So, if you don't want to continue after your 60 days of checking us out, you give me your kit - or what is left of your kit. I will personally write you a check for the $75 you invested in your distributor kit, okay?

"No hard feelings. You can't make an intelligent long-term decision about our business until you try it out. Don't worry about me either. I simply mail the kit back to the home office and they will reimburse me the $75. It is easier if I do it for you since I am in contact with the home office weekly. And it's easier for you too. You won't have to wait for a refund.

"And finally, don't feel bad if this opportunity isn't for you. It is not for my Mom, my two best friends, and my next-door neighbor either. You just have to check it out for yourself to know if this is going to be your big break in life or not. Fair enough?"

Wow!

This is the way to tell our skeptical prospect about our money-back guarantee. We bring it alive. We make it believable. And we get a chance to sneak in a great benefit - that this opportunity may be the big break in our prospect's life.

Finally, if we think this is being too soft on our prospect, it is because we are looking at this situation from our point of view. We are a distributor already. It is easy for us to overlook the risk of joining.

So, let's put ourselves in our prospect's shoes. Let's take away the prospect's risk of making a bad or foolish decision. Instead, we will now make joining our program easy.

MOTIVATION FROM WITHIN.

Yes, we can influence our prospect's motivation with contests and incentives.

However, motivation is easier when it comes from inside. When our prospect has strong core values and desires, sacrifices are easy.

Sometimes we hear a prospect say, "Sure I want to be in my own business, but I can't afford the $60 distributor kit."

Really?

Your prospect may be short on cash, but how motivated is your prospect?

Consider the following summary of a story in *Chinatown: A Portrait of a Closed Society* (HarperCollins, 1992):

"Many immigrants start out as street peddlers for three or four years until they have saved enough money (between $50,000 and $100,000) to start their own small business. The book tells about Lin who earned $360 a week peddling vegetables, fruit, and umbrellas. His annual income: $22,000. What is amazing is that Lin saves $18,000 of his income and lives on the other $4,000.

"Lin has saved over $70,000 in four years so he can start his own business."

Hmmm. Lin is motivated. He is ready to make a few sacrifices in his standard of living to achieve his dreams.

Now, back to our original prospect who couldn't come up with the $60 investment for his distributor kit. What do you think? Does this prospect have a strong, burning desire to have his own business?

People take too many things for granted. We are spoiled. We want things, but aren't willing to pay the price. Immigrants also want things, but they are willing to pay the price. They are happy to have the opportunity to pay the price.

What do average people want?

- They want to be the boss, but refuse to stay late after work.

- They want to take exotic vacations, but refuse to save anything from their monthly paychecks.

- They want to own their own business, but only if it is free.

- They want to be a network marketing leader with a five-figure monthly income, but they can't get away from personal activities to attend opportunity or training meetings.

No wonder **average** people have trouble building a networking business.

They must build the business themselves, and that is a gross inconvenience. That is why successful networkers look for the un-average person. It is easier to build a successful network marketing business when somebody is working with internal motivation.

So how do we change a prospect's internal motivation? How do we change our prospect's vision of his future?

Let's take a look at motivation via goal-setting.

GOAL MOTIVATION, THE DOWNSIDE.

How about those goals? Great things, aren't they?

Did you set New Year's goals? Have you kept them? Whoops.

Did you ever make ambitious plans and fail to follow through? Whoops.

Setting goals is fun. However, having a goal is **not** motivation. A goal is just a target or direction for our efforts.

Have you ever seen distributors do this?

First, they spend a week formulating their goals. Then, they purchase a goal planner manual to organize and prioritize their goals. Visualization? They spend a month cutting out pictures and pasting them on poster boards in their homes.

What is next? These distributors enroll in a goal-setting program. The seminar approach should bring out the best in their goals. After the seminar, they should reformulate their goals with this new, additional information. Then they must break down their big goals into smaller goals. Next, the weekly goal support meetings start. When the group gets large enough, they qualify for the group rate on the advanced goal workshop.

The story goes on and on and on. They are so busy setting goals, refining goals, discussing goals, that ... well, you get the picture.

The point is, it is hard to motivate a distributor by saying,

"Go set some goals!"

The world is full of people who have great goals and no results. Goals point us in the right direction.

However, goals don't provide the "kick in the behind" action we need to move forward. It is too easy to just set goals, not achieve them, and forget about them.

New Year's goals versus New Year's activities.

As you know, we are strong advocates of activities. Too many distributors set goals and think that they have actually done something. All they have accomplished is a "wish list" that they gaze upon during the commercial breaks of their favorite television shows.

But don't get us wrong. Goals do have a place in our businesses. They help us select which activities we should concentrate on. And, goals help us see opportunities that can move us closer to our goals. Too many times we work hard, appear busy, but never achieve network marketing success.

Why? Because we are doing the wrong activities. For instance, here are a few activities that can take time away from sponsoring activities:

- Arranging products on our shelves.

- Re-reading the policies and procedures to understand the fine print on section 13.

- Putting fresh pages in our organizers and presentation books.

- Polishing the presentation white board.

- Calling other distributors just to visit and rehash the last opportunity meeting.

- Memorizing the ingredients in each product.

- Writing flyers to insert into catalogs or prospecting packages.

- Taking goal achievement courses over and over again.

- Writing detailed explanations of the finer points of the compensation plan.

- Planning the next training session that the same old crowd will attend.

- Chit-chatting with unmotivated prospects on the Internet.

These activities are **nice**, but they won't help us reach our **goal** of building a large and successful network marketing business. Completing activities is great. But let's make sure we are working on the **right** activities!

"SETTING GOALS IS EASY. ACHIEVING GOALS IS DIFFICULT."

We hear the same thing from the gurus, the self-appointed experts, the trainers and the local big mouth at the bar:

"You have to set goals. That is the key to motivation."

Right. Sure.

If setting goals was the key to our motivation, then we would all be super-motivated now, right?

Well, we **aren't**.

You see, it is easy to set goals. Every year we set goals for the New Year, to earn more money, to exercise, to lose weight, to be more loving, to win the local tennis tournament, to wake up an hour earlier, to sponsor more people, to spend more time with the kids ...

Hey wait! This is just a list of some of our goals that we didn't achieve.

And that is the story of our lives. We all set goals. That is the easy part. Setting goals is no problem at all.

The **problem** is that we seldom **achieve** these goals.

Does this sound like you? Like your downline? Like your prospects?

I bet it does. Because failing to achieve our carefully-planned goals is just human. We mean well, but we consistently fail to achieve our goals.

Why is this?

Why do we just make a list of our shortcomings and then set goals to fix them? Unfortunately, there is a reason we have shortcomings in our lives.

We have shortcomings because those things are hard for us to do!

I will give you an example.

I am fat because I love eating at pizza buffets much more than I like to exercise. For me the choice is easy.

Choice #1: Leisurely load my plate with multiple mouth-watering varieties of pizza, and then enjoy an eating experience … or,

Choice #2: Change clothes, drive to a local gym, sweat, strain, and work myself to a painful exhaustion.

The choice is clear. Pizza rules. And donuts come in as a close second place.

So, what should we do?

We don't want to waste our time talking about setting goals. That is the easy part. We all have plenty of experience **setting** goals. Setting goals is more like a "wish list" of things we always wanted to do, but didn't.

Instead, let's concentrate on **achieving** goals.

Wouldn't it be nice to consistently achieve goals? Or help our downlines consistently achieve their goals?

Sure it would, but the solution to this problem has to be **simple**. Really simple.

Because if we have to follow multi-step, complex formulas, then we would have plenty of time to fail. We need a solution that is quick, easy to implement, and will work.

So what we need is the "Big Al" Three-Step Formula for Goal Achievement.

THE "BIG AL" THREE-STEP FORMULA FOR GOAL ACHIEVEMENT.

Three steps. That seems simple enough. Let's get to work. We need to break the cycle of setting goals and not achieving them.

Step #1: Choose a goal.

Picking the right goal makes a difference. We want a goal that is:

A. Simple to understand and easy to achieve. We need to build up some goal-achieving muscles, so let's start small. Let's set a goal that is easy, really easy. If we achieve that easy goal, we will have confidence that we can do this again, maybe with a slightly harder goal.

B. Within our control. If our goal was to sponsor five people this month - this wouldn't be within our control. We can't control other people and what happens in their lives. However, we can control the goal of <u>talking</u> to ten people this week. Let's choose a goal that is totally within our control and doesn't depend on others.

Okay, so let's start with a sample goal. Here are some easy examples we could choose from:

- Start a conversation with one stranger a day for one week.

- Wake up every morning 15 minutes earlier.

- Walk one mile during lunch every day this week.

- Don't watch the depressing news channel for two days.

- Read one chapter of a personal development book before work every day this week. Chapters too long? Okay, start with two pages a day.

- Eat only one donut for breakfast instead of two.

- Create one new friend this week.

- Pass out a sample of your product every day for one month.

- Eat one healthy meal a day.

- Send one email a day to a friend, just to say "Hi" and renew your relationship.

Pick a goal for yourself right now as we go through this process.

Back in 1999, I picked a goal of losing 29 pounds (13 kilos) in 90 days.

I will use that goal as an example as we go through these three steps.

Okay, now we have our goal. What is the next step?

Step #2. Pick a penalty.

Let's get motivated – emotionally. Reward motivation is nice, but having to pay a penalty? That is emotional.

Finding the right motivation is one key to achieving goals. Without motivation, we simply waste time drawing graphs, putting up pictures of things we will never achieve, reading more books, breaking more promises ... well, you get the picture.

Elegant, neat, pretty theories and 17-step formulas look great in books, but they don't work when you have challenges that test your motivation.

Yes, we can put a time limit on this goal, make it specific, devise little sub-goals, and do all the stuff that helps. However, we have to look at the big picture first. We did these things before, and we didn't achieve our goals.

Setting the goal is no big deal. Anyone can do that. What we need to do now is find out ways to motivate us to **achieve** that goal.

Everyone has a preferred method of motivation. I am sure there is no single right way for everyone.

Here are some common motivational techniques that we use for setting our goals, but that have limited effects.

- Attitude motivation. Yes, I could listen to motivational audios and read motivational books. Maybe I could add some subliminal recordings too. Actually, I have tried these things, and yes, they do make me feel better about not achieving my goals.

- Changing my self-image. I could chant affirmations, meditate, visualize and more. This is powerful, but is much easier to talk about than to do. Usually this takes a lot of time and effort. This will be much too complicated for most of us because we are conditioned to want results right away. We frequently don't have time to gradually change our self-image. The goal we chose may have a short time limit.

- Faking enthusiasm. You know what I am talking about. Jumping off chairs, cheering, smiling ridiculously, and becoming hyperactive. Usually we do this to impress others, but there is no real change in us as a person.

- Placing a picture of me turning down a donut on my bathroom mirror. Sure, I have a picture of working towards achieving my goal, but this doesn't give me the emotional determination to actually achieve the goal.

All of these techniques are good, but not powerful enough to guarantee that we will work hard to achieve our goal. We know that logic is nice, but emotion is what drives us as humans. If we are going to change, if we are going to get motivated, we need **emotional** reasons.

The list of motivational techniques we have discussed so far doesn't give us a deep, passionate emotional drive. That is why these techniques don't work.

We need a highly emotional reason to achieve our goal. Then, our goal will be easy to achieve.

So the technique that we are going to use to reach our goal is ...

Blackmail!

Yes, that's right. Blackmail.

If you read our book, *Sponsoring Magic*, you know that the **fear of loss** is always **greater** than the **desire for gain**.

For example, we are extremely motivated to avoid paying an expensive speeding ticket. Maybe we will take a half-day off work, hire a lawyer, drive down to the county courthouse, and fight the judicial system to avoid the speeding fine.

Yet, we won't spend an extra hour on the telephone prospecting for new distributors, even though that extra hour could earn us hundreds of extra dollars.

Fear of loss is always greater than the desire for gain.

So, if I am going to get maximum motivation, if I am going to overcome my exercise aversion, and if I am going to reduce my chocolate intake by three or four pounds a week, then I will have to use this fear of loss motivation tool.

Here is how it works.

I have to choose the **penalty** if I don't achieve my goal. And this **penalty** must create an excruciating emotional pain in my life.

Let's pick a penalty that is so painful that I will be sure to reach my goal.

Here are some ideas.

If I don't reach my goal of losing 29 pounds:

- I have to go and socialize at my worthless cousin's New Year's party. (I hate to socialize. I hate my worthless cousin. But I could suffer for a few hours.)

- I have to personally paint the house. (This is a big job. I would hate it. But it's not painful enough to give up chocolate.)

- I have to go shopping with my wife for seven consecutive days. (Oooh. This one really hurts. However, I guess I could read a book while waiting for her to browse through merchandise.)

- I have to eat eggplant and broccoli every day. (Yuck! Disgusting stuff. But maybe if I closed my eyes and quickly swallowed I could get through this ordeal.)

What's happening here?

None of these penalties are big enough or severe enough to get me motivated to lose weight now.

I need a bigger penalty.

If the penalty isn't big enough, this technique won't work. It has to be a big, big penalty.

So what would be the most evil, distasteful, disgusting, wretched penalty I could think of? What penalty would be so terrible to me that I would start losing weight immediately? So terrible that I would even lose weight while on a cruise ship?

What penalty could be that bad?

I chose this:

I would have to donate $1,000 to the Bill Clinton Legal Defense Fund!

Ooooooooh! Now that's bad.

That is so bad that I instantly lost my appetite!

I can't think of anything worse than donating 1,000 after-tax dollars to a politician's lawyer. I don't care that much for lawyers either.

To donate $1,000 to the Bill Clinton Legal Defense Fund would just about kill me. This is truly blackmail of the lowest kind.

And it worked!

I lost those 29 pounds in 1999 just in time to avoid my penalty. Nothing took my eyes off my goals.

When my Democratic Party friends offered me free chocolate, my emotional feeling towards my penalty made me say:

"No thanks. I don't have an appetite right now. In fact, I am feeling a bit queasy."

If I was sitting by the 24-hour ice cream machine on the cruise ship, I thought:

"No way! 1,000 hard-earned after-tax dollars to a lawyer? No way! No way! No way!"

What about you?

Are you thinking of a possible penalty for not reaching your chosen goal? I hope so.

Penalties work.

And if you have chosen your goal and penalty already, then you should be feeling pretty emotionally motivated now.

But what about Step #3?

The final step is to announce your goal and penalty ... **publicly!**

That's right. We could easily keep our goals a secret, just in case we decided they were too hard. Then, no one would know that we quit and gave up on our goals.

However, we want the emotional support of our friends to motivate us to achieve our goals.

Plus, we want the emotional non-support of our so-called friends who will taunt us and challenge us to reach our goals.

Can you see my semi-friends saying this to me in support of my weight-loss goal?

"Hey, chubby! Have some more ice cream. Bill Clinton's lawyer needs a new swimming pool!"

Or maybe I get that midnight call from an unidentified caller who whispers, "Pizza ... pizza."

Cruel semi-friends. But, this motivates us to reach our goal. We don't want them to be right.

So announce your goal and penalty to the world!

The more you announce your goal and penalty, the more committed you will become. To avoid personal embarrassment and the dreaded penalty, you won't let anything get in your way.

Will this work?

Only if we use it.

So here are the three steps.

#1. Set the goal.

#2. Set the penalty.

#3. Let everyone know the goal and the penalty.

We are now on our way to achieving our goal. Remember, anyone can set goals. That is the easy part.

Separate yourself from the masses by actually achieving your goals.

"LET'S PRETEND" GOAL-SETTING.

It is hard for our new distributors to feel motivated if they don't have goals. Goals don't motivate, but goals do give direction. Goals point distributors to where they want to go and to what they want to accomplish.

This isn't a goal-setting book, but if our distributors don't have goals, how can we motivate them? That would be telling a new distributor, "Hurry up. Go! But I am not sure which direction you should go ..."

Let's get some direction first.

So, we ask our new distributors, "Please write down your goals."

The distributors stare at the paper. Nothing is written. Why?

Why do distributors avoid setting goals?

Maybe our distributor is thinking, "What if I fail? Am I thinking too big? Will someone laugh at my goals?"

My friend Lloyd Daley offers this solution. He simply uses these words:

"Let's pretend."

He asks the new distributors to suspend reality and just pretend that anything is possible. For example, the new distributors could write "Let's pretend" at the top of a piece of paper. Next, the distributors make a list of wonderful things that could happen if they were pretending. Maybe the list could look like this:

Let's pretend:

- My mortgage is paid and I could spend that mortgage payment on shopping and golf. I could shop on Saturday and Sunday when things are on sale. And I could golf Monday through Friday when the golf courses aren't crowded.

- I drive a new luxury mini-van that holds all of my son's tennis gear. We follow other parents around the country to different tennis tournaments throughout the summer holidays.

- I sell my alarm clock to my neighbor. Every morning I still wake up at the same time out of habit. I make my cup of coffee, and then sit outside my front door and wave to my neighbors going to work.

- My family finally takes the dream vacation of a lifetime to Disney World. We create memories of a week-long stress-free holiday while staying at the Disney Resort.

- My bonus check covers all my monthly bills. Now I can compose music every morning while looking out the window at my garden.

- Once a month, our family takes a four-day holiday, camping at a different national park. Our new camper will have everything we need, except the actual campfire.

- I take a holiday in Paris. While touring one of the local museums, I take time out to write a postcard to my negative former co-worker. I say, "I wish you were here with me now. Maybe next year? Let's visit over coffee when I fly back home."

This easy "Let's pretend" mindset will get our new distributor writing goals quickly. Now we can point our distributor in the right direction.

It is more practical to motivate our new distributor if he is pointed in the right direction.

Is this the only way to get distributors to write down some goals?

Of course not. This next method is more involved, but very, very effective.

25 THINGS.

Many years ago, Art Jonak taught me this technique.

We sit down with our new distributor and say, "Please write down some goals for your new business." And, what happens next?

The distributor stares at that piece of paper. Nothing happens. The distributor is scared to write down any goals. Why?

The distributor's subconscious mind is working against him. His subconscious mind is saying, "You've never succeeded at anything before. I have over 1,000 examples in our life where you failed to achieve what you wanted. Don't write anything down. You will only disappoint yourself. You will be setting yourself up for failure. Save yourself from embarrassment. Leave the paper blank."

No amount of logic can change this situation. The subconscious mind is working against us.

But what if we could get the subconscious mind to work **for** us instead of against us? Now, that would be powerful.

We will trick the subconscious mind with the following statement:

"25 things I am going to do AFTER I become a Diamond Executive."

Imagine that Diamond Executive is a good leadership position in your company. Maybe a Diamond Executive will earn $5000-$10,000 a month. Now, that is a lot of extra money in addition to one's monthly salary. We could do a lot of fun things with that much extra money every month.

Here is what happens when the new distributor says, "25 things I am going to do after I become a Diamond Executive." The subconscious mind takes over. The subconscious mind says, "Of course I can do all of these wonderful new things if I'm **already** receiving that much extra money every month."

Now, the subconscious mind removes the limitations. We are not asking the subconscious mind if these wonderful things will come true or not. We are only asking the subconscious mind to list what could happen if we had all that extra money.

Now the magic happens.

The new distributor starts listing all the wonderful goals and desires from deep within his mind. Here is an example of what someone's list could look like.

25 things I am going to do AFTER I become a Diamond Executive.

1. Buy a new car for my spouse.

2. Take French lessons.

3. Fly to visit my grandchildren every month.

4. Retire my spouse from work.

5. Install new landscaping.

6. Hire a maid to clean three times a week.

7. Take skydiving lessons.

8. Hire a cook for Fridays and weekends.

9. Take a round-the-world cruise.

10. Go on a charity mission for three months.

11. Send both daughters to private school.

12. Travel to all the "away" games of my favorite sports team.

13. Buy a farm and move back to nature.

14. Homeschool the children and take them to visit countries instead of giving them geography lessons.

15. Remodel the house and get new furniture.

16. Go back to college and finish my humanities degree.

17. Take a four-day family holiday weekend every month.

18. Take Formula One racecar driving lessons.

19. Purchase the family home where I was born.

20. Visit the 20 largest shopping malls in North America.

21. Take a two-week "cousins" trip with my favorite cousins.

22. Open my own Pilates studio and coffee shop.

23. Go whitewater rafting in Alaska.

24. Visit Milan and attend a fashion show.

25. Invest in stocks and bonds like my brother-in-law.

Usually it takes 15 or 20 minutes to finish this list. Once finished, make some copies. The new distributor can carry the list, put a copy on the bathroom mirror, even post a copy on the refrigerator.

When a skeptical neighbor comes to visit, the neighbor can see the list of goals on the distributor's refrigerator. After seeing the goals, the neighbor understands why the new distributor is so passionate about his new business.

You will want a copy also. When your new distributor becomes discouraged, all you have to do is remind the new distributor of one or two of the goals on this list. You can say, "I know you don't want to come to Saturday's training, but you do want to send your daughters to that private school, right?" Now it is easier for the new distributor to gather the courage to overcome the obstacles along the way.

The bottom line? By tricking the subconscious mind, we can help our new distributors set meaningful goals immediately.

But we have to do our own list first.

When I first heard this technique, I was excited to get my distributors to do it. I could picture myself saying to them, "Please fill out your list of 25 things right now." Then, they might ask me, "Can I see your list for a moment? Maybe it would give me some ideas on how to start."

Now, it would be embarrassing for me to say, "Oh, I didn't fill out my list yet. I just wanted you to fill out a list."

So for this technique to work, that meant I would have to fill out my list first. That is exactly what I did. After filling out my list of 25 things, I posted my list on the Internet. Two days later, 26 members of my downline had posted their list also. Four days later, 56 people had posted their list on the Internet. The momentum was building.

It became fun to say to distributors, "Let's see your list." To be part of the "in crowd," everyone wanted to have their list.

So our advice? Fill out your personal list first. Then it will be easier to get your downline to duplicate your example.

"IF IT DOESN'T WORK — I QUIT."

New distributors have weak commitments and convictions. They give up when someone tells them "No."

Ever hear this conversation? Your new distributor complains:

"I talked to my three best friends at work. They didn't want to join, and didn't even want to try the product. This business doesn't work. 100% of the people I've talked to so far have turned me down. I don't think this business is for me."

It is easy to give up when our commitments are small.

But imagine this. What if your new distributor invested $300,000 to open a restaurant in his neighborhood? Do you think he would complain and say:

"My three best friends at work didn't come and eat at my restaurant when I opened it this week. I want to quit. This is too much work and I hate it when people who should come to my restaurant ... don't come."

Of course he wouldn't say that. With $300,000 invested, I am sure your new distributor would put up with friends not coming, relatives not coming, unmotivated staff, city taxes, bookkeeping, insurance, bad weather and a host of other problems.

Why?

Because investing $300,000 is a much bigger commitment. When we are committed, we can handle rejection and problems. We won't give up at the first little issue.

Now, our new distributor hasn't invested $300,000 in our business. However, we can still make the business appear huge in his mind.

How? By reinforcing how big this business could be for our new distributor. For example, we could say:

"When you get this business right, you could earn enough to leave your job, spend time with your family, and earn more than your boss. Now, learning and building this business won't happen overnight. Depending on your skills and commitment, it could take a few years.

"So let me give you the good news and the bad news.

"First, the bad news. In the beginning, you will experience lots of discouragement and seem overwhelmed. There is so much we don't know when we start. And it will take time for people to feel comfortable with you in your new business. They won't join or buy right away. They will want to wait and see if you are committed over the long haul. So it might be months before your friends and relatives join or buy from you.

"Now for the good news. You don't have $300,000 at risk. You have only put a few hundred dollars into your business. If you can be patient and learn new skills, then in time, people will trust your commitment to your new business. Then it will start getting easier and easier every month.

"Just think how long it takes to become a professional basketball player. You might spend ten or 15 years learning and practicing your skills before you earn your first paycheck. But in network marketing, you can learn how to build your business in just six months. You don't have to wait years for a payoff from your efforts."

"But I need to earn money right away."

Make sure that we are clear on this. We offer to teach them how to do our business in six months. We are not guaranteeing that they will be earning large checks in six months. They still have to work their business.

"But what if I fail?"

Let's relieve our new distributor's fear of failure by telling this little story.

"Imagine you were on a date. The food was bad, the movie was bad, and you didn't relate well with your date. Would you give up dating for the rest of your life? Of course not. You would continue dating. The rewards of a great relationship outweigh the temporary failure."

Our prospects and distributors worry about temporary failure. Our little dating story helps them understand that if their initial efforts fail, this failure would only be temporary. By continuing to work, they can be successful.

Stories can help new distributors have realistic expectations. Without stories, many distributors would quit at the first sign of rejection.

We want our distributor to stay with our business long enough to learn effective skills.

Why stories?

Stories go deep into the minds of your prospects and distributors. We communicate better with stories. People who listen to a story actually create a movie of that story in their minds.

We can remember stories from our youth, but we can't remember a history date 15 minutes later for a history exam. Some stories are so powerful that they will eat at the inside of our brains until we do something about that story!

Stories move our emotions. That is why we cry at movies, or listen to gossip.

Think about your company conventions. So many leaders will parade on stage and tell their personal story of failure to success. We identify with these speakers, and inside, a little bit of us changes from every emotional story.

Motivational books, inspirational audios, and attending live events help to change the internal motivation of distributors. (Just one of many reasons live events, rallies, conferences, and conventions work so well.)

Yes, there will be problems.

Success in business does not come from lack of problems. All businesses have problems.

Once our new distributor understands and expects these problems, these problems won't become roadblocks. Our job is to give our new distributor some realistic expectations so when these problems happen, it will seem normal.

Let your new distributor know that people are skeptical and hesitant to make decisions. It is normal for people to change their minds or fear change in their lives. So in the beginning, expect problems such as:

- Telephone calls not returned.

- Appointments cancelled at the last minute.

- People saying they want to "wait and see."

- Best friends who won't be supportive.

- Orders cancelled.

None of these events are big enough to affect a new distributor with commitment.

That is our job as leaders. To help motivate our distributor to have a commitment that is bigger than the problems he will encounter along his journey.

WHEN YOU HAVE A DREAM.

"When you have a dream, nothing gets in your way. And when you don't have a dream, everything gets in your way."

—Tom Paredes

As network marketing leaders, we spend hours, days, and even weeks trying to solve problems and eliminate challenges for our distributors.

No matter how much we clear the road for success, a negative-minded distributor will still find more obstacles.

We waste time. We can't win. And we bite our lips, stand by the sidelines and watch the negative-minded distributor fail.

Why do many potential superstars fail?

Because their dreams are smaller than the obstacles they encounter.

This also explains those "rags-to-riches" stories. These people didn't allow any obstacle to get in their way.

Their dreams were far larger than the obstacles they encountered.

The lesson?

Our future leaders need a **dream**. If they don't have a dream, we will waste our time helping them overcome the daily obstacles of business. They will always require our assistance.

Instead of trying to fix obstacles, we should help our future leaders create a dream.

How a dream can motivate distributors.

My good friend, Tom Paredes, tells the story of a lady from the Dominican Republic, a small island in the Caribbean. This lady had a dream. She dreamed of living in a better home, sending her daughters to private school, buying a car, and building a better life for her family.

She joined a network marketing company that sold water filters. The water filters sold for about $120. That was the average income for a family for an entire month in her area.

Do you see a problem?

One water filter was an entire month's salary for a family. How could anyone afford to purchase her water filters? With only $120 a month to cover food, shelter, and clothing, there was no money left to purchase a water filter. And with no bank accounts or credit cards, this was not the ideal place to be selling water filters.

However, this lady had a dream.

Her dream motivated her to find a solution. She was pregnant, did not have a car, yet she was able to become the #1 water filter salesperson in North America for her company.

So how did she do this?

Every day she would go to a poor neighborhood. That was not hard, as all the neighborhoods nearby were poor.

She would get 12 families together. Each family spent $10 so that they could have a water filter for their neighborhood. During the month, these 12 families would share this one water filter. One family kept the water filter in their home. The other 11 families would come daily to get clean water for their families.

The following month, the same families would pay $10 more to purchase another water filter for their neighborhood. Now they had a second water filter that they could all share.

These families continued paying $10 each month until each family had their own personal water filter.

How many poor neighborhoods could she talk to? Unlimited. That is how she became the number one salesperson for water filters in North America.

When people have a dream, nothing gets in their way.

Use this dream to motivate distributors to their full potential.

WHY PERSONAL DEVELOPMENT TECHNIQUES ARE LIMITED.

There is more to motivation than a positive attitude. In everyday situations, we need to be more proactive in motivating our distributors.

Read on.

Book and audio motivation.

I love books and audios.

Let's see how book and audio motivation works with our de-motivated network marketing distributors.

Imagine our first-level distributor feels depressed and wants to quit our business. It is time for us to reach into our bag of motivation tricks and pull out a ... book?

What are we going to say to our depressed distributor?

"Here, read a book. You need some personal improvement."

I don't think a wave of instant motivation will come over our depressed distributor. In fact, he might think,

"Hey! You read the book. It is your business. I quit. I can't do this anymore. It is not working. In fact, you can take this book and ..."

Well, we get the message.

If reading a book was the secret to motivation, then "speed-reading" graduates would be instant leaders. They aren't.

Giving a book or audio is a nice gesture, but it **isn't** the ultimate solution to motivating our team.

Maybe the book or audio will help with our depressed distributor's attitude.

However, attitude means **how** we look at something. Attitude is not action.

Motivation by example.

We still want to motivate our unmotivated distributor, right? Let's look at the following scenario.

We have a brand-new distributor named Tony. Now, we know that Tony worked hard all month long. Every day Tony gave recruiting presentations, retail presentations, made new contacts, and asked for referrals. However, Tony ended up with **no** distributors, and **no** retail sales. Although he worked hard, he failed to produce any results.

We are Tony's sponsor. We know it is our job to lead and motivate. So we decide to motivate Tony by **example**.

The next morning we telephone Tony and say,

"Hey Tony, guess what! I worked hard all month. I gave recruiting presentations, retail presentations, made new contacts, and asked for referrals. I got a $10,000 check ... and you didn't. I feel pretty good about the business. I feel pretty positive. I earned $10,000 ... and, well ... you didn't. So follow my **example**. Be positive, sponsor a lot of people, make a lot of retail sales, and be successful like me. Go out there and get them, rah-rah-rah."

Can you imagine what Tony is feeling? Anger and jealousy. He has fantasies of an upline assassination. He mumbles to himself,

"Sure, if I had a $10,000 bonus check I would feel motivated too. Just give me the $10,000 check **first**."

Yes, we set a great personal example. We gave recruiting presentations, retail presentations, made new contacts, and asked for referrals. We were positive. We were motivated.

However, our excellent personal example did nothing to improve Tony's lack of motivation. In fact, we may have de-motivated Tony a bit.

Motivation by enthusiasm.

Let's change our approach and use some enthusiasm. We will try the same scenario again. Tony gives recruiting presentations, retail presentations, makes new contacts, and asks for referrals. Again, Tony ends up with **no** distributors, and **no** retail sales.

What is our new strategy?

Massive personal enthusiasm.

We telephone Tony and say,

"Hey Tony. Guess what? I got a $10,000 check and you didn't! Yep! It is great having a great big check like this!

O-o-o-h let me tell you, it is absolutely terrific, I am so excited! Yes! Yes! Yes! O-o-o-o-w-e-e! You know Tony, if you got some enthusiasm, you could get a $10,000 check too. Go for it Tony! Rah-rah!"

What is Tony thinking after our enthusiastic phone call? Tony is thinking that his (expletive, expletive, expletive) upline sponsor should move to a much warmer climate.

Enthusiasm is nice, but it doesn't solve Tony's problem.

Attitude motivation.

Attitude is pretty important stuff. It has been said that attitude makes the difference between success and failure. Well, let's put this attitude theory to the test with Tony.

Tony works hard giving recruiting presentations, retail presentations, making new contacts, and asking for referrals. Again, Tony ends up with **no** distributors, and **no** retail sales.

What is our newest strategy?

Attitude adjustment.

We telephone Tony and say,

"You know what your problem is Tony? You need a **better attitude!**"

We can easily imagine Tony's acid reply.

Attitude works best when it comes from the inside. It is hard for us to press a new attitude on someone else.

Now, we can help change Tony's attitude over time. That is what personal development does. But in Tony's case, we don't have much time. He is on the verge of giving up. Tony will look at every attempt to motivate him with a slightly negative viewpoint, so we have to be good.

So what else could we try?

Motivation by recognition.

Many people work **harder** for personal recognition than they will for money. Let's put this motivation by recognition idea to the test. We feel that if Tony could get a little recognition, he would feel better about moving forward.

How do we think the following scenario would work at our next monthly meeting?

We stand in front of 100 enthusiastic distributors at our monthly training meeting. Next, we clear our throat to get the audience's attention, making sure everyone will notice Tony's moment of recognition. We say,

"Ladies and gentlemen. I would like to introduce someone to you tonight who has worked hard the entire month. He has worked harder than anybody I know. He gave a multitude of recruiting presentations and retail presentations. He made new contacts and asked for referrals. Unfortunately, he didn't sign up a single new distributor. He failed to make a single retail sale. And after a full 30 days of hard work, well, he completely failed in every activity he tried. So at this time I would like to recognize the hard-working ... Tony!

"Let's give him a big round of applause. Tony, stand up and wave so everybody can see you!"

Tony fails to respond positively to his embarrassing moment of recognition. Later that evening we narrowly miss becoming the victim of a hit-and-run accident in the parking lot.

Okay, a bit exaggerated. But even if we give Tony recognition for a tiny step forward, Tony might still feel embarrassed. We need to make a huge motivational difference in Tony's life, and this may not be enough.

What should we try next? Remember, motivation is one of our duties as a leader.

Find their dream motivation.

Let's go back in time to the early 1900s. Several top psychologists discovered some interesting things about personal motivation. They found that to motivate a person, we must first recognize **what that person really wants.**

In network marketing, we call this, "Finding their why until they cry." We want to find out what they want so badly that this would create an emotional experience for them.

Now, we might find ourselves thinking,

"Gee, that makes more sense than those other techniques such as fear motivation, bribery, goal motivation, or recognition. They didn't seem to work. They had limited effects."

Let's put this new "Find their dream motivation" theory to the test with our unmotivated, discouraged Tony.

Imagine we are visiting Tony and his wife, Vera, at their home. We say,

"I know you are both feeling a little down. It is not often that a full month's work goes unrewarded. However, let's put last month behind us and look ahead.

"Tony, when people feel discouraged, they often find it helpful to focus on their dreams. What do you want from your network marketing business? What will you do with the money you will earn?"

Tony answers,

"I want a car. I want a new car from my efforts in this business. Now I feel embarrassed every time I park my car at work. Everyone else has a new or better car."

This should be exciting. This should be motivation at its finest, right? We just discovered what Tony wants: a car.

Now, with our amazing discovery, we believe that Tony should be ecstatic. He should be full of energy, jumping up and down and running out to sponsor people. With our new-found information, we wait for Tony to jump in the air, glow with confidence, and levitate.

We look at Tony's wife, Vera. She sits calmly in her chair. We look at Tony. He sits in his chair. In total disbelief, we realize that Tony **is still not motivated.**

What is wrong here? We found out **what** Tony wants from his networking business, but nothing is happening!

Maybe Tony is just a fluke, an exception to the rule.

Still concerned about their motivation, we turn to Vera and say, "Vera, what do you really want from your network marketing business? What will you do with the money you will earn?"

Vera answers,

"I want a new house. A big house. Maybe even a mansion. I grew up living in rented apartments. I want to feel good about myself as a homeowner."

Then, **silence**. Nothing happens. Both Tony and Vera sit calmly in their chairs staring at us. There is no clapping, no cheering, no smiles, no excitement, and no motivation.

Nothing has changed!

We invested time, energy, and brain power to find out what they wanted. Nothing happened.

Finding out someone's dream is nice, but it seldom motivates people to take action. It is better than ignoring our distributors, but we need more motivational options in our arsenal.

Maybe those psychologists in the early 1900s weren't so smart after all.

Show them how to get motivated.

Suddenly we realize,

"Gee, I am doing this all wrong!"

A bright idea hits you head-on. Now we know what makes the difference. It is not **finding out** what the distributor wants, the secret is ... to **show** the distributor how to get it! Now that makes a lot more sense!

Anyone can dream or fantasize. The motivational difference? Maybe people want to know how to achieve their dreams. If we show people how to get their dreams, we can motivate them, right?

Let's put this technique to the test.

We will now show Tony how to get that new car. We say,

"Tony, if you want a new car, you have to go downtown to a new car dealership. A salesman will help you pick out the colors. The sales manager will settle the pricing. And, the finance manager will put you deeply in debt with payments for 72 months.

"Or, if you want our network marketing company to pay for your new car, you need to get on the telephone every night and cold-call strangers until you make enough sales every month to qualify."

Done. We accomplished our goal. We **showed** Tony how to get a new car.

Tony stares at us like we've lost our mind.

Motivated? No.

Tony sits in unmotivated shock.

Showing Tony how to get that new car didn't motivate him. Maybe this "show them how to get their dreams" technique will motivate Vera.

We say,

"Vera, let me show you how to get a big house, a mansion. First, you search the Internet for the local real estate sites. Pick a real estate office. Find an agent with a nice name. Then, arrange for the agent to show you some big houses. That is their job, you know, showing people houses. Anyway, when you see a big enough house, you sign a contract and go for it!"

Whew! That one was a little tougher, but we did **show** Vera how to get a big house.

Vera continues to sit quietly. Maybe she is holding her excitement inside. Then again, maybe she doesn't want Tony to go out and get another month of rejection for his efforts. She is tired of listening to Tony complain about his lack of success.

We are now looking at two of the most **unmotivated** people we have ever seen in our entire networking career. We have tried our best to motivate them, but none of the previous techniques worked.

One better solution.

We think,

"If I have to motivate people as one of my sponsorship duties, I want something that is going to work more often! I don't want to waste my time with techniques that only work in limited circumstances. I want a better way to motivate my distributors."

Showing distributors "how to get what they want" just doesn't seem to work quite the way we thought it would. So we re-think what we know about motivating distributors.

Finally, we figure it out! We clearly see a better way of motivating distributors. Motivating is **not** "finding out what distributors want," and it is **not** "showing them how to get it."

A much better way is ...

HELPING people get what they want.

Mothers know this secret instinctively. Maybe they have a built-in motivation gene. Mothers know how to motivate.

For example, a two-year-old child is playing with his toys in the living room. The toys are everywhere. The sofa is covered with toys. Toys are underneath the coffee table. There is even a "toy mountain" in the middle of the living room.

The two-year-old child is small. The living room is big. To the child, it appears that his whole universe is covered with toys.

Now, his mother says,

"Time to pick up your toys."

The child looks around and thinks,

"Oh my! My whole universe is covered with toys. There is no way I can pick up all these toys. I am not experienced at this. The job is too big. What if I fail? Isn't there a government agency that will do this for me? This is discouraging. I don't even feel like trying."

In other words, the child is very **unmotivated**. So, what does his mother do? She turns to her husband and says,

"Will you get down on your hands and knees, and help our child clean up the toys?"

The husband kneels down and starts throwing the toys into the toy box. The child looks around and thinks,

"Hey, Dad is helping. He is pretty good at this. I've got

some experienced help here. Dad has done this a few times before. He is big, and seems to be pretty strong, so I think that between the two of us — we can do it! I think he is a pro at this!"

The two-year-old child begins throwing some toys in the box because he is **motivated.**

He knows he can get the job done before he turns ten! Why? Because he is receiving experienced **help** (Dad).

(There is also a message here on how mothers are great trainers. They train dads and children. However, that is another story for another book.)

Can this **helping** motivation technique get the same results in network marketing? **Yes!**

The new distributor panic attack.

When a new distributor starts in network marketing, what happens?

He looks at all the activities and processes needed to conduct his new business. Presentations have to be made. Ouch! That is a lot of memorizing. Cold calls and recruiting appointments sound scary too. And, have you ever looked at how complicated a product order form can be?

Then, the new distributor must master public speaking, accounting, management, leadership, public relations, sales skills, and ... this can be overwhelming. In fact, the new distributor's **entire universe** is covered with **hard-to-do** projects.

The new distributor looks at these tasks and ... **panics!**

"Oh no! Sales presentations, appointments, retailing, and what's that coefficient of the dynamic enzymes that go through the flushing system? It is all so overwhelming!"

The solution to the panic attack? Simple.

Offer a helping hand.

The sponsor offers to help the new distributor. The sponsor says,

"Hey, don't worry. We will learn this business one step at a time. Just look at this as on-the-job training. First, let's do this. I am going to make a couple of prospecting phone calls. All I want you to do is listen. Then, after you feel comfortable, you can make a phone call or two. I will listen in and help you with any questions the prospect might have."

Now the new distributor thinks,

"I have an experienced person helping me do this! Now I know I can do it!"

Motivation can make the difference in any new distributor's career. And, motivation can be spelled: **H-E-L-P.**

This **H-E-L-P** motivation can work anywhere. Let's take a look at another example of **H-E-L-P** motivation.

Janitor woes.

Imagine there was a big sports event at our city's 100,000-capacity jumbo stadium. The stadium is packed. The fans are rabid. The teams are evenly matched. Then, in the crucial closing moments of the game, one team cheats — and wins.

The fans go **crazy**! Half the fans are celebrating. They are throwing gum wrappers in the air. They are dumping soft drinks on the fans in front of them. They are cutting up the seat cushions and throwing the pieces into the wind.

The other half of the fans are **furious**. They start fights in the stands. They dump trash on the opposing fans. They stick their chewing gum under the seats. The entire stadium becomes one large riot.

Now imagine it is the next morning and you are starting a brand-new job as janitor of the city's jumbo stadium. **Groan**. It is just you, your bucket and your broom against a stadium trashed by yesterday's riot.

On a motivational scale of one to ten, how do you feel? About zero. You look at the riot debris and think to yourself,

"This is a mighty big job. My entire universe is covered with garbage. What if I fail? Isn't there a government agency that will do this for me? This is too discouraging. I don't even feel like trying."

The boss strikes back.

Just then your boss appears (that is, your sponsor if you are following this network marketing analogy). Your boss realizes that you need motivation.

The boss attempts some fear motivation and says,

"If you don't do your job and clean the stadium, you are fired!"

Well that certainly **won't** motivate you as you think,

"Hey, you can't fire me — I quit!"

Next, your boss tries bribery since you're not motivated by threats. He says,

"Instead of making $15 an hour, if you do a good job today and for the next six months, I will raise your salary to $15.05 per hour."

Again, your motivational levels remain at "low."

Want to give goals a shot? As you survey the undeclared disaster area, your boss says,

"I know what you want. You want to finish the job, right? That is your goal. So go for it! Get to sweeping!"

Yeah, right. Big deal. You begin to yawn with boredom.

Maybe recognition would work better. Your new boss says,

"So you got the janitor's job! Oh my goodness. I had that job for 25 years! I am sure you will become well-known as the Janitor of the Jumbo Stadium."

Boy, just what you need. Recognition as the janitor of the city's jumbo stadium.

Or, how about using some example motivation? Your boss says,

"After 25 years as the janitor of this stadium, my boss promoted me to foreman!"

Do you feel motivated? No.

Let's try some enthusiasm motivation. Your boss cheerfully announces,

"Man, am I ever glad that I don't have your job!"

Well, **your boss is motivated**, but you still remain unmotivated.

Hmmm. That still leaves the attitude approach. Your boss says,

"Hey, you have an extremely bad attitude about this janitor's job. I suggest that you change your attitude. You know, shape up or ship out!"

Yes, you do have an attitude about this job, and it certainly isn't changing with this kind of motivation.

Maybe a little find-out-what-you-want motivation will work.

Your boss says,

"I bet I know what you want! I bet you want to clean this stadium, right?"

Brilliant. Your boss's IQ is now approaching double digits.

But what if your boss were to show you how to get the job done? Your boss points to the top row of the jumbo stadium and says,

"See that top row? What you need to do is start way up there, start cleaning row by row. When you get all the trash and debris to the bottom row, start hauling it away in trash bags."

Well yes, the boss did show you what to do, but it still looks like too big of a job for a brand-new employee.

The boss gets smart.

None of these traditional methods of motivation are working. So, let's try our new motivation technique of **H-E-L-P**.

Your boss taps you on the shoulder and says,

"Hey, I used to have that job and it is not as bad as it looks. As a matter of fact, let me help you. Since it's your first day I will show you my fast-clean system, and by 2:00 p.m. we'll be finished! You will be amazed. Then, we will go eat some pizza or something!"

Now, what happens to **your** motivational level? Maybe it is not at "10," but it's a whole lot better, isn't it? You feel more confident when you have an experienced helper who has successfully completed the task before. Your confidence goes up. Your motivation goes up. Your working activity goes up. Hey, this **H-E-L-P** motivation really does work!

Putting this H-E-L-P motivation to work in our business.

Now, back to our networking business. If we have an unmotivated distributor in our group, what can we do to change his motivation level?

Maybe we can call our distributor and say,

"I will tell you what: if you set two appointments, then I will set two appointments. I bet we can get a few new distributors signed up before this weekend. That will get your group-building off to a fast start."

Our previously unmotivated distributor is now thinking,

"My goodness, my sponsor is a real pro! I have been in the business only two weeks! What an opportunity! What great upline support!"

Now, doesn't this method of motivation work better than calling our new distributor and saying:

"Have you sponsored anybody yet?"

We will raise our new distributor's motivation by continuing to help build his business. What if we call our new distributor and say:

"Remember Judy, the person we signed up earlier this week? Well, I helped Judy yesterday and we signed up two more distributors. You now have two new second-level distributors!"

Now your new distributor is really getting excited!

All we are doing is helping our distributors reach their goals, helping them build their business.

Want to get your new distributor even more motivated? Try this. Call your distributor the next day and say,

"Remember those two new second-level distributors? Well, I went with one of them and we sponsored three more people. You now have three new distributors on your third level!"

H-E-L-P is a great method of motivation. If we don't use the **H-E-L-P** method, it is like saying,

"I hope every new distributor I sponsor is personally motivated, has perfect knowledge of our business, exhibits exceptional selling skills, has a business degree, loves rejection, and is an all-around super individual."

If that is what we expect from new distributors in our networking business, then we should open a Fantasy Land amusement park instead.

Using **H-E-L-P** motivation is why the Big Al two-on-one sponsoring system works so well. This technique is covered in my book, *Sponsoring Magic*.

A final scary thought.

Many times we can change our distributors' motivation levels by simply **helping** them build their business.

So, what will you think when you hear a network marketing sponsor say,

"My group is just a bunch of unmotivated jerks!"

Whose **fault** is it?

The group ... or the sponsor?

HOW TO PRE-MOTIVATE YOUR PROSPECT AND OPEN UP HIS MIND.

In my book, *26 Instant Marketing Ideas To Build Your Network Marketing Business*, we wrote about a survey form technique. Here is the basic idea of how it works, but then, let's take it a step further. Let's review.

Did you ever bring a guest to an opportunity meeting?

While waiting for the opportunity meeting to start, what goes through your guest's mind? Negative thoughts? Thoughts of resistance and fear?

Maybe your prospect is thinking this, "Oh my. What did I do? Why am I here? They are going to try to sell me something. Better put up my defenses. It could be a pyramid operation. Why did I get tricked into coming here? How do I get out of here alive? I am in a den of shark-eating salespeople. Better put on my frown now. I need to think of some killer objections. Better protect my wallet. Oh, I better look bored and non-interested also. Be careful. Don't let them talk me into anything!"

This isn't starting well, is it?

Would you like to motivate your prospect to have an open mind? A great attitude? An eager desire to join your business? And do this all before your opportunity meeting even starts?

Here is a technique that uses a simple survey form. Any distributor can use this form. No skill needed. Just give the prospect the form.

This form changes your prospect's attitude from negativity to "looking for possibilities" when your opportunity presentation begins.

What happens when you bring a guest.

Remember all those negative thoughts in your prospect's mind while he or she waited for the opportunity meeting to start?

Are these the thoughts you want your prospect to have?

Of course not.

Instead, when the first speaker begins you want your new prospect to be thinking:

"I am looking for an opportunity ... now! I want a career change or at least a part-time career that is interesting and actually pays me what I am worth. I need something for my retirement. I need to get ahead in life and my job just gets me by. I want a lot more. In fact, maybe there is a way I can quit my job. I want a lot more from life so that I can travel, but I don't have a plan to get there. How can I solve these money problems and get what I want in life? I sure hope this meeting has a solution for my problems."

That is the attitude you want your prospect to have when the opportunity meeting begins. Now, how do you create this attitude?

All you need is a simple form.

Before we go to the form, let's look at one other problem that doesn't help our prospect. The problem?

We take our benefits for granted.

We have so many good benefits. We don't talk about them long enough for the prospect to internalize and appreciate each benefit.

For example, we talk about time freedom. We mention how the prospect won't have to go to a job. How the prospect can have more time with his family.

Or we may talk about money freedom. We tell the story of how the prospect will have enough money to pay the bills with money left over to take holidays and enjoy life.

However, during an opportunity meeting, the speaker quickly mentions time freedom and money freedom in one sentence. He might say:

"Good evening, ladies and gentlemen. Thanks for coming. Tonight we are talking about time and money freedom. Let me tell you a little bit about the Wonderful Corporation. The Wonderful Corporation was started in 1972 by Mr. Wonderful himself, etc, etc, etc."

Because the speaker mentions these two benefits so quickly, these benefits don't affect our prospect. Our prospect never gets the chance to think about what time and money freedom can mean to him.

What if we could get our prospect to contemplate and internalize these two benefits, time and money freedom, before the opportunity meeting begins?

What if our prospect took ten minutes before the meeting to think about what time and money freedom could mean to him?

Wow!

Now when the opportunity meeting starts, our prospect is thinking:

"Gosh, I want to quit my job. I want to retire and spend more time with my family and hobbies. However, there is no way I can retire with my present job. I will have to work until I'm 85 years old! I sure hope this opportunity meeting tonight will have a plan or idea on how I can achieve time and money freedom!"

With this kind of attitude, our prospect has an open mind and is looking forward to tonight's opportunity meeting. Our prospect is looking for a solution to his time and money freedom problem.

And, we have the solution.

How can we get our prospect to think like this?

By giving our prospect a special survey form to fill out before the opportunity meeting starts.

Here is a sample of what your form could look like.

Name: _____

1. **When would you like to retire?**

    ☐ In one year   ☐ In two years

    ☐ In five years   ☐ In ten years

    Great! Please write down your plan to achieve this goal.

2. **How much money do you need monthly to retire comfortably?**

    ☐ $2,000   ☐ $3,000

    ☐ $4,000   ☐ $5,000 or more

    Great! Please write down your plan to achieve this goal.

3. **How much money do you need to invest at a 6% return to receive your desired monthly income? (Take your answer from question #2 and multiply by 200.) Please write down your amount below.**

    Great! Please write down your plan to accumulate this money.

We arrive 15 minutes early for the opportunity meeting. As soon as we sit down with our prospect, we can pull out a copy of this form and say:

"This form is for your own personal use. Nobody else will see it. This will give you some ideas about what to look forward to in our opportunity meeting this evening."

Your prospect starts to fill out the form and thinks, "Hmmm, fill in my name. That's easy enough."

And then the fun begins.

Your prospect reads question #1: "When would you like to retire?"

His answer?

"Oh, I would like to retire in about five years."

Then the hammer drops when he reads:

"Great! Please write down your plan to achieve this goal."

Now your prospect is stunned. He must contemplate and internalize this question and construct a workable plan. Your prospect thinks:

"Hmmm, I guess I could start saving for my retirement now, but I am already two payments behind on my car.

"And, my VISA is over the limit. I can't live on what I earn now, so I couldn't take a cut in pay if I retire.

"And if I did retire, who would pay me anyway? I am too young for social security or pension payments, and that doesn't amount to much anyway. I would have to have a lot of money in the bank to be able to retire.

"Maybe I could get a part-time job at a fast food restaurant. No, that won't work. Those jobs are already taken. I don't know what to do. There is no way I can retire in five years. In fact, I will have to work until I am 90 years old!

"I don't have a plan to retire. I don't even have a hope of retiring ever! Retire? Are you kidding? I can barely live now!"

Your prospect wishes he could retire, but realizes he can't. Now the impact of time and money freedom is internalized. Your prospect understands that unless he comes up with a plan, he is doomed to working forever.

Your prospect doesn't have a workable plan. He doesn't even have an unworkable plan!

At least question #2 is a bit easier.

Next your prospect reads: "How much money do you need monthly to retire comfortably?"

Let's say that your prospect thinks:

"Okay. This is easy. I can retire on only $3,000 a month. I will live in a little log cabin by the lake and spend my retirement fishing. I can eat the fish, chop wood for heat, and I can get by okay if I just have $3,000 a month."

And then your prospect reads: "Great! Please write down your plan to receive this monthly income."

This is a killer dilemma because your prospect has no plan. He thinks:

"How can I get $3,000 every month? If I quit my job, my pension and social security benefits won't come close to what I need. Plus, I won't even qualify for them until I am too old to enjoy them. The local high school students have all the fast food restaurant jobs locked up. I am not a rock star, so I can't expect any royalties from a hit album.

"Maybe I can talk my boss into paying me a salary and I just never show up to work. No, that won't work. The company is downsizing and I think I will be the first casualty anyway.

"I don't have any stocks and bonds, so I won't receive monthly dividends. Hey wait! This is terrible! Just how do people retire anyway? How do people get money in their bank account every month if they don't have a regular job? How can anybody retire?"

Your prospect is getting desperate. His lack of a workable plan to retire is now very apparent.

And finally, question #3.

Your prospect reads, "How much money do you need to invest at a 6% return to receive your desired monthly income? (Take your answer from question #2 and multiply by 200.) Please write down your amount below."

We call this the "Rule of 200." It is an easy way for people to realize the large amounts of cash they will need to retire comfortably.

In your prospect's case he thinks:

"Okay, if I want to retire on $3,000 a month, then I multiply $3,000 by 200 and the answer is … $600,000!!! Yikes! That's a lot of money!"

In total shock, your prospect reads the last sentence: "Great! What's your plan to accumulate this money?" Now your prospect begins to feel totally discouraged. He thinks:

"$600,000 is a lot of money. Let's see now, I have $1,000 in savings right now. At six percent interest, that is about $60 in interest a year. Divide that by 12 months and I would receive about $5 a month in interest income. That leaves me about $2,995 short of what I need.

"But wait. I am two months behind on my car payments and over the limit on my VISA card. I will have to use that money this month for the bills. Yikes! Now I don't have anything.

"Maybe I can get adopted by rich, sickly parents? No, not much chance of that happening.

"I tried winning the lottery. Sounded like a good plan but all I did was lose money.

"I don't have a plan. I don't have any hope of retiring in five years. I sure wish I had a plan. **I sure hope that the opportunity meeting this evening gives me an idea of a plan that might solve my problems.**"

Now your prospect is sitting on the edge of his seat with the proper attitude. He is thinking: "Let me look for reasons why tonight's opportunity will work instead of looking for reasons why tonight's opportunity won't work."

The difference is amazing.

When the meeting starts, your prospect is not fighting or resisting your opportunity. Instead, your prospect is looking for **reasons to agree** with your opportunity.

Open-minded prospects make sponsoring enjoyable. The secret to changing your prospect's attitude is easy. Just use a simple form.

But what if I don't use opportunity meetings?

You can use this form anywhere. Use your imagination. Here are a few ideas:

- At a trade show, pass out these forms with your telephone number and a brochure.

- For advertising responses, mail a copy of this form with your follow-up package.

- Use this form at in-home meetings and during one-on-one presentations.

- Put this form on your website.

- Pass out this form at your company's Christmas party. That should get the conversation going. Of course, that might take away from the other employees' temporary holiday cheer.

- Use this form as part of your distributor training sessions. This will give them a reason to stay in your business.

With a little imagination or editing, you can use this form technique to solve many of your sponsoring challenges.

But what about young people? Not every prospect is old.

This form won't work for every prospect. For instance, if your prospect is 18 years old, retirement seems 100 years away! An 18-year-old prospect doesn't care about retirement.

What do young prospects care about? Young prospects don't want to work 45 years like their parents. So now we create their form to look like this:

Name: _____

1. **When would you like to quit your job, and start enjoying life?**

    ☐ In one year   ☐ In two years
    ☐ In five years   ☐ In ten years

    Great! Please write down your plan to achieve this goal.

2. **How much money do you need monthly to replace your current take-home pay?**

    ☐ $2,000   ☐ $3,000
    ☐ $4,000   ☐ $5,000 or more

    Great! Please write down your plan to achieve this goal.

3. **How much money would you need to invest at a 6% return to replace your current monthly paycheck? (Take your answer from question #2 and multiply by 200.) Please write down your amount below.**

    Great! Please write down your plan to accumulate this money.

Well, that was fun. Younger prospects are generally more positive and open-minded. They haven't been beaten down by society and a dream-sucking vampire boss yet. They will enjoy the form and start dreaming.

Isn't that a good state of mind for a prospect?

But what about retailing products or services?

Of course. Why not? We can customize this form for anything.

Let's do a sample form for dieting.

Name: _____

1. **When would you like to reach your desired weight?**

    ☐ In one month   ☐ In three months
    ☐ In six months   ☐ In one years

    Great! Please write down your plan to achieve this goal.

2. **How much weight will you need to lose safely every month?**

    ☐ 3 lbs.   ☐ 5 lbs.
    ☐ 8 lbs.   ☐ 10 lbs. or more

    Great! Please write down your plan to consistently achieve this goal.

3. **What different major lifestyle, exercise, or eating habits will you utilize to lose this weight safely?**

    Great! Please write down why this time will be different from previous diet attempts.

So have some fun. Make your own forms and watch how your prospects improve their attitudes and open their minds.

Let a simple form pre-sell and pre-motivate your prospects.

MOTIVATION BY ASSOCIATION.

There is an old saying, "If you hang around four broke people, I guarantee you will be number five."

"I am 55 years old ... and depressed."

Your distributor feels like giving up hope. That is easy to do. Why?

Many of our beliefs come from experiences. If a different dog bites us every week, it won't take long to develop the belief that dogs are dangerous.

So let's look at Carl's life.

Yes, my friend Carl is depressed, very depressed. He is 55 years old and has a net worth of ... zero.

It is not his fault.

His car payments, credit card payments, health club dues, yearly vacation, and expensive mortgage use up his entire salary. He can't save a single cent. He is lucky his company will provide him with a pension at age 65.

And that is why he is depressed.

His company pension and his government retirement benefits total only 65% of his current income.

Not bad, but here is the reality of his upcoming retirement.

He can't live on 65% of his present food intake.

The bank won't reduce his car payments to only 65% of his present payment.

His vacations will still cost the same.

He won't be getting any discounts on gas and utilities.

His clothing purchases will still be at full price.

In other words, Carl's income will be reduced by 35% the day he retires. However, his expenses won't be reduced 35%.

In just ten years, Carl is going to be miserable.

Network marketing to the rescue?

I want to help Carl. He is my friend.

So during lunch one day, I showed him how network marketing could add a little income to his life. I know Carl doesn't want to spend much time building a business. So, I only presented Carl with a simple part-time plan with modest income goals.

I showed Carl how to earn an extra $400 a month. That is a believable figure in Carl's mind.

Carl's response?

"$400 a month! You have got to be kidding! That would barely pay the interest on my monthly credit card bills! That is not enough to change my retirement situation. It is just not worth the effort. I won't sacrifice my limited free time for only $400 a month."

And Carl is right.

If Carl would save the $400 in extra income every month for his retirement, well, that wouldn't be too exciting.

In just ten years Carl's extra retirement fund would be worth only $48,000, plus a little compound interest. Maybe a grand total of $60,000.

While $60,000 is quite a bit of extra money, the reality is this:

$60,000 at 6% interest will only produce a monthly income of $300 a month.

An extra $300 a month is nice, but it won't solve Carl's problem. No wonder Carl can't get excited about investing his free time to build a part-time networking business.

Even if you added the $400 monthly network marketing check to his $300 interest income at age 65, this would only add $700 extra a month to his pension. While that amount is sizable, Carl would still have to struggle to make ends meet.

What can Carl do?

Carl's plan is to hope that things magically change. He feels hopeless. He believes his problem is outside of his control.

Things don't magically change, so what else can happen?

1. Carl can get depressed even further. He can't see a way out of his current financial situation.

2. Or, we could use our experience and imagination to come up with a plan of hope, and maybe that could motivate Carl to move forward.

Here is the plan I suggested to Carl.

1. Invest the extra time to build a part-time $400-a-month network marketing income.

2. We will find a house in Carl's neighborhood that is for sale. We think we can get a house down the street for about $200,000.

3. Get ready for a fun retirement in 10 years.

Carl has some equity in his home. He could use the equity in his present home for the down payment.

Carl's monthly payment including taxes and insurance would be $2,700 a month for ten years.

The good news is that Carl could pay off the house in only 10 years. It would be a wonderful asset for his retirement.

The bad news is that Carl can comfortably rent the house for only $2,300 a month. It would take an additional $400 a month from Carl's pocket to pay the monthly mortgage payment.

And that is where Carl's part-time network marketing business fits into his retirement program. This is the source of funds he needs to purchase and pay off the house.

So, if Carl starts his network marketing business and purchases the house, how much will this add to his retirement income?

In ten years, Carl's investment house should be worth about $300,000. That's adjusting for only minimal inflation. And this $300,000 house will be fully paid off.

A $300,000 investment at even a low 5% return equals an additional $1,250 a month to Carl's retirement.

But wait, there's more!

Carl will still be getting his $400 a month network marketing check, so his total retirement income will be increased by $1,650 a month! Remember, this $1,650 is in addition to his government pension and company retirement pension.

Now that is exciting.

And it can all happen in just 10 short years.

It is hard to be motivated when we don't have a solution.

We can motivate people when we educate them with options that give them hope.

Do you know anyone who is age 55 and who would like to receive a $1,650-a-month pension increase?

I do. I know lots of people like Carl.

But the reality is ...

Carl won't start a small network marketing business.

Carl won't purchase that house down the street.

And Carl will suffer and be miserable in his retirement.

Why?

Because Carl has 55 years of programming that makes him believe:

"I am a professional victim. There is nothing I can do to help myself."

And this is the ugly truth when we talk with prospects like Carl. We are fighting 55 years of bad programming, and that is pretty hard to overcome in just one visit.

So what can we do to help the Carls in the world?

We can give them some new programming. We can show them new information that will gradually help them believe that they can do something to help themselves.

You could use the book, *Why You Need to Start Network Marketing* to help change Carl's viewpoint. It is only a short book, about the length of Carl's attention span. Or, pick another book to broaden the possibilities in Carl's mind. How about an audio? Or take Carl to a "live" seminar?

Why not take Carl with you when you visit your positive friends? Their "can do" attitudes will help wear away Carl's negativity.

Then, pass on small success stories when you visit with Carl. Adding these real-life case studies makes it harder for Carl to continue saying, "Oh, none of those things work."

And never tell Carl what to think.

What Carl thinks and believes is up to him. Only he can decide to change his beliefs.

Not everyone is ready to be motivated right now. Some people need more education and more hope first.

So don't start giving them presentations. Instead, give them new information that will help them change their negative belief system.

- Loan them a book.
- Loan them an audio.
- Help them associate with positive people.

And then, in a few months you will have lots of great prospects. These prospects believe they can do something to help themselves. These prospects can be motivated. And these prospects are ready to take action.

"WHAT MOTIVATES PEOPLE TO MAKE THOSE DECISIONS?"

People don't go out of their way to make bad decisions. Yet sometimes we might wonder:

1. Why do people act the way they do?

2. Why do people make silly decisions that we can't understand?

3. Why do prospects avoid our money-making opportunity?

Because people make decisions based upon their personal value system.

People don't go out of their way to make bad or illogical decisions. They make the best decisions they can - based on the values they put first in their lives.

Since each individual is unique, everyone has slightly different values and goals. That means most people won't look at or judge opportunities the same way we do.

Instead, they will use a completely different standard to decide what is best for them.

We all have different values and different standards.

Understanding how our prospects **prioritize** these values will be critical on our path to motivating people.

When we understand which values are dominant in people's lives, we can then understand and better motivate them by respecting their needs and desires.

Let's get started by investigating some common values. As we learn about these values, just think how each value gives a different point of view to almost any situation.

Reality can change drastically when viewed through different values.

Value #1: Power.

John organizes the church choir and the local homeowners' association. These are not elected positions, he simply assumed them. When John wants to get projects done, he doesn't hesitate to assign duties to anyone and everyone.

Is John satisfied with the results of his delegation? No. John feels he could have improved on every outcome with more personal intervention.

John doesn't listen to critics. He strongly believes in what he does, and how he does it. If you wanted to get something done, you would call on John. He sees the big picture (with him on top) and won't let frustrating circumstances, regulations and negative people stand in his way.

People who are focused on power are assertive, confident, and productive. They are strong organizers and supervisors. Decisions are fast and certain. They are also controlling, nosy and bossy.

They are also never wrong. Just ask them.

With energy to spare, people who value power like to delegate jobs and tasks to others but are rarely satisfied with the results. They always want and expect the best.

Power people are always looking for new opportunities to gain more power. Changes of jobs are common if the new position offers more power, authority or control. Money takes a secondary role in the decision.

You can find power-motivated people as leaders of the church choir, politicians, and officers in organizations. They love to give meetings and won't back away from a challenging situation.

Motivating John is easy. John naturally wants to organize, control, and tell others what to do. He will focus on building his group so that he ranks high as a leader. Then he can have the platform and status to be in charge.

We can start John's excitement early in his career by having him be the master of ceremonies at the opportunity meeting or training. Or maybe have John organize and run the monthly training meetings.

An early taste of power will get John focused on building his business fast.

Let's look at our next value.

Value #2: Financial security.

Steve is only $1,000 in debt. This bothers him so much that he takes a job as a part-time taxi driver to pay off this debt.

He drives a sensible car, rarely eats out, wears conservative clothing, and has a reliably stable job with the government. With savings accounts in two different banks, Steve feels obligated to make regular deposits from his bi-weekly paycheck.

Steve saves his frequent flier miles from business trips and uses them for his holidays, and often integrates business meetings into those holidays for tax purposes.

Steve concentrates on financial security and accumulates lots of assets in bonds, CDs, etc. He is safety-conscious and conservative. The mere thought of bouncing a check can give him a panic attack. He carefully accumulates money for the future, while postponing the small luxuries that can make life easier.

Avoiding risk is extremely important in both his financial transactions and his personal relationships. Steve considers how every decision will affect an uncertain future.

People like Steve take part-time jobs so that they can contribute more to their retirement fund. Look at loyal employees who stay with one company. These people will often talk about money and are always open to new ideas for financial independence. You can find them cornering financial consultants at parties.

Now, what would be exciting to these "accountant-thinking" individuals?

Residual income!

When they calculate how much money they would have to deposit in the bank to get the same financial return, they almost pass out with excitement.

Constantly remind these individuals of their growing residual income. This will keep them focused and motivated.

Value #3: Desire to be rich.

Carol lives in an exclusive apartment complex. Her apartment is furnished with top-of-the-line appliances, an entertainment system, and is fashionably decorated. Every week she has a housekeeper come in. She routinely meets with her personal shopper.

All of her credit card balances are high and she has very little in savings. She spends money on lottery tickets and betting pools.

Recently, on two weeks' notice, Carol moved halfway across the country for a new job with higher pay and better benefits. Before long, Carol, a highly social person, is well-connected with people all over the city.

People like Carol have the philosophy that if you look like you have wealth, and live like you have wealth, someday you will surprisingly wake up with wealth.

They buy expensive clothing and jewelry on credit cards. Luxury salesmen love them as they lease big luxury cars and join the elite country clubs so they can have lunch with their idols.

Like those who value financial security, this group often talks about money. However, instead of discussing how to gain money, they talk about how to spend money.

Exact figure amounts (the higher the better) of their latest new boat, car, or house pop up frequently in conversation. A big motivating factor is envy of others and keeping up with the Joneses.

As aggressive risk-takers, they put money in high-risk stocks and other high-earning (if unstable) investments.

They can be hard workers if the job looks prestigious enough to complement their lifestyle. They are open-minded to new opportunities that will help them achieve their goals.

So what motivates this type of individual in network marketing?

Think about winning the luxury cruise or company trip, getting an overpriced watch, the big car ... oh, and dressing up for the banquet.

Value #4: Desire to look good.

Tim is a gym fanatic who works with his personal trainer five times a week. He is not a professional body builder, but takes six different herbal steroids and weight-gaining protein formulas every day.

He has regular monthly appointments to get his hair cut and colored (along with his beard) and a manicure. In his bathroom are seven types of shampoos and conditioners and four different styling formulas for his hair. The stylish gym bag and bottom drawer of his office desk each have duplicate sets of his haircare products.

Focused on the appearance of their bodies, people like Tim spend all their time and money going to health clubs, spas, and salons.

This used to be primarily a woman's value, but today more and more men are joining them. We have all seen the increase in ads for men's hair coloring, belly-busters, etc. It is not a bad thing. Vanity has now become an equal opportunist.

My daughter, Ann, says that it may be good for men as it will make them appreciate what women endure in the name of beauty. Of course, men will never truly understand a woman's plight until confronted with a full leg wax ...

People who value personal appearance have work schedules that compete with the spa appointments and workout sessions. Their first loyalty is to their physical appearance, so they are receptive to opportunities that would enable them to enhance their appearance.

Attention to detail is another trait they embody, as well as a tendency towards perfectionism.

You won't find this group working where store uniforms are mandatory. Designer clothing and smart dressing are the norm. The key word in their vocabulary is "accessorize." Look for the stylish watch, bracelet, or pendant and don't forget the oversized ring. (Please note: engineers and accountants seldom have this value high on their priority list.)

If you asked someone from this group to speak at your meeting, they would first want to check the lighting in the room to make sure they would look good.

What motivates the vanity crowd?

Meeting prospects for coffee at a trendy restaurant, dressing up for the formal evening banquet at the convention, and showing their new look from the front of the room when they qualify to speak. Qualify to speak?

Yes, simply let them know that if they reach a certain level of accomplishment, they will be the focus of everyone's attention by being the speaker.

Ready for another value?

Value #5: Loving relationship with their partner.

James is a newlywed. He and his wife, Sara, have just bought their first home and spend most weekends working on the renovations together.

Although they often have friends over, they rarely go out for the evening. James has a stable job but is constantly looking for new opportunities to improve his and Sara's lifestyle.

They take off several days a month to spend quality time at home with each other, but make up the work on lunch hours. They rarely take business trips and avoid work-related dinners and events.

People who prioritize a loving relationship with their partner rely heavily on their mates for decisions. They are rarely seen alone. You can find them kissing in public, wearing matching outfits, and holding hands. They call their "significant other" 12 times a day from work. You can hear them when you pass their office door making smoochy noises into the phone.

Co-dependency makes their relationship work. They make slow, calculated decisions while taking into account how it will affect their partner. They work hard but are not work-obsessed. Finding a line between work obligations and personal life is important to them.

If you want to be nurtured, this group makes a perfect upline. Not only will they call you regularly, but they will listen to your personal problems and opinions for hours. They are the ultimate support system.

However, the downside is that they dislike making new contacts outside of their comfort zone. Just think of the word "cocooning." They fit that description.

I bet you can think of several people who have this value at the top of their priority list.

This group values their relationships with their fellow distributors. Group outings, social evenings, and group bonding events will keep them motivated. Video conference calls are more for the bonding experience rather than for training or prospecting.

And now for yet another value.

Value #6: Family.

Paul is a family man with four children. He makes certain he attends their Little League games, recitals, plays, swim meets, Christmas concerts, fundraisers, and parent nights. Every night the family sits down for dinner together and talks about everyone's day.

Paul can change a diaper, fix a leaky sink, call a plumber, and brandish barbecue grill tongs with authority. The house is always bustling with kids, two dogs, a cat, and a goldfish named Squeak. He and his wife take the family out to the lakeside cabin for two weeks every year.

Family-oriented people have priorities and values that come before work. The majority of their time is devoted to the family. Family vacations and dinners are important to them.

They are loyal and can be motivated by opportunities that will benefit the family. Decisions are ponderous as they will discuss decisions with every member of their family including the fourth stepcousin twice-removed living in Europe.

You see them at Disney World with an extended family group of 200 - all wearing identical T-shirts with "Reunion Tour" on them.

Commitments mean a lot to this group. Long-term goals and relationships come easily for them too. This group is especially popular with grandmothers, but not so popular with teenagers.

Look to people who have "family" at the top of their values for stable and consistent leadership.

And with their family reunion skills, they make great organizers for your next training or regional event. They will even get their family to volunteer to help.

A huge motivating factor in their lives is the time freedom that network marketing can provide. More time with the family ... exactly what they want.

So when the company announces an incentive trip, see if that trip will allow other family members to come. Family trips? Excellent motivation.

The next value?

Value #7: Career fulfillment.

Michael powered his way through college and found a good job with opportunities for advancement. Since then he has changed jobs once, and only then for a nearly identical position with a larger company.

He and his wife communicate largely by phone and email because he is often on the road for business trips or spending evenings and weekends at the office.

Although he is very successful and the youngest vice president in the company, Michael is still frustrated with his progress in the company. Michael's schedule is fast-paced and high-stress. He receives pressure from work and compounds it with pressure he places on himself.

Because of his career goals, he refuses to take time off to relax and regroup. Instead, Michael relies on pain relievers for his chronic migraines and visits the chiropractor. (Gee, a perfect candidate for a nutritional products company.)

People focused on career fulfillment are often workaholics whose time is focused on getting ahead, getting the promotion, and being handed the key to the executive washroom.

Where do you find them?

You can sometimes catch a glimpse of them on planes, buried under files and pounding furiously on a laptop. They feel undervalued at work and believe their efforts lack acknowledgement and appreciation.

New opportunities are not always considered unless they lie directly in the pre-mapped business plan they have made for themselves.

Leadership is easy for them as they are quite willing to set the example for the group. You won't have to call them to remind them of an upcoming opportunity meeting.

You can only hope your best distributors have this value higher on their priority lists. When a person has this value high on their list, you can stand out of their way, as they don't need you interfering with their plan. They are pre-motivated for maximum time investment into their career.

Value #8: Desire to feel needed.

Cathy is a second grade teacher. She volunteers at the local hospital and works with the youth group at her church. Her husband owns a business and she takes care of the books and payroll. Every day she makes lunches for her children and drives them to and from school. In addition, she has an extensive network of close friends who rely on her for advice, favors, and as a general sounding board.

People who want to feel needed are always willing to give you the shirts off their backs in return for a smile and a pat of appreciation. They can sometimes become martyrs.

They willingly make sacrifices for everyone and actively seek acknowledgment. Many are social workers, volunteers, charity workers, and hospital staffers.

Because they like the responsibility, people who value their usefulness are efficient and productive. They are loyal friends and employees. If you wanted to delegate a monthly newsletter project to someone in this group, you would know that the project would shine with excellence.

I am sure you see many people in your life who have this value high on their list. Some super-moms are a natural with this value.

The more assignments they can assume, the more motivated they become.

Ask yourself, "What projects would these distributors support?"

An example? Organizing the monthly banquet. The logistics of the banquet are easy, but wouldn't it be great if someone called fellow team members and reminded them to sponsor someone now, so they could qualify to come to the banquet?

Value #9: Personal enlightenment.

John would rather meditate than watch cable television or play video games. He has checked out every philosophy book on the Internet and is an avid attendee of self-development courses.

Understanding who he is and how he fits in the universe is more important than money, job promotions, weekend sports and lawn care.

People focused on personal enlightenment are intent on "finding themselves." You can find them in New Age bookstores, yoga classes and self-help workshops. Their audio library is all about simplifying their lives and understanding the universe.

Because their personal journeys of exploration offer them positive rewards, they spend lots of time and energy sharing their insights with others.

Alternative careers blend well with their lifestyle. Sometimes they will take on odd jobs to move away from the rat race. They are often open to new ideas, but if they are looking for the child within, don't offer to babysit.

This group possesses incredible teaching and explanation skills. They can decipher complex information and present it clearly and with insight. If they give a lecture on a subject that interests you, it will be a fun learning experience.

This group values network marketing as an alternative lifestyle and also as a personal growth experience. So don't make them memorize the compensation plan.

Allow them to make their network marketing career part of their personal growth experience.

Our favorite task to keep these people motivated and engaged? Have them lead a mastermind or book-reading group that meets weekly by telephone or video conferencing. They love the subject matter, and they have to coach others to master what they have learned.

The best way to learn things is by teaching those things. This activity helps them master more skills to become more effective leaders.

Ready for another common value?

Value #10: Adventure/travel/ adrenaline junkie.

Pat lives for the next quest, escapade, and journey into the unknown. He has started several businesses over the years but has abandoned them one by one for long-term adventures around the globe.

Once it was a six-month endurance challenge to Antarctica and beyond. Another time he explored southern Asia on a mountain bike for almost a year. He knows bits and pieces of several languages - most of it consisting of phrases requesting beer and bathrooms and a few to compliment the women he meets.

The adrenaline junkie misses meetings because he's off on a whim. He's moving double-time through the airport to catch a flight to Africa, planning to hunt lions – barefoot, with a pocketknife.

He is easily influenced by new ideas. When a new obsession hits, he takes off full-force and focuses all his energies on it.

Highly productive, he charges through new projects. On the downside, he also has a short attention span and needs a constant source of new challenges.

He can tell you where to get the best cup of coffee in 58 countries. He enjoyed parachuting over Guam, rock climbing in the Andes, scuba diving with the sharks, and crossing a busy street in New York City. He is very spontaneous.

As distributors, people like Pat surge ahead with tremendous growth and momentum. However, unless there are new challenges, their energies will quickly turn to the next adventure.

This group is hard to keep focused on the long-term building of their groups. You will have to step in and develop stable leaders under the adrenaline junkie.

My favorite adrenaline junkie is Mike. I have known Mike for over 25 years, and through about 25 career changes and changes of addresses.

For the first ten years, I tried to get Mike to become a boring, stable person. But, I was acting from **my** values. Needless to say, I was always frustrated and scratching my head whenever Mike threw away security for a new risky adventure.

I didn't get it.

Then, after ten frustrating years, I got it.

It was all about which values were most important to Mike!

He was making intelligent choices based upon his priority of values. All of a sudden, I understood Mike, and appreciated him even more as a friend.

He was true to his values.

Once we understand other people's values, we understand their decisions. That lesson freed me from frustration with others. I learned to allow people to have their own values which, of course, dictated their decisions.

Make sure to keep introducing new adventures and new challenges to keep these adrenaline junkies motivated in their network marketing careers.

How about another value?

Value #11: Aim for fame.

Jerry was once near a crowd that saw former President Clinton walk to the podium. When Jerry meets a new person, he says,

"When President Clinton and I were in Tampa, Florida back in 1998 ..."

Jerry loves to drop the names of anyone famous and hopes their reputation will rub off on him. Look inside Jerry's house and you will see every trophy and award he's ever won displayed in his living room. There is even a copy of his kindergarten graduation certificate complete with two gold stars for coloring inside the lines.

People looking to become famous save every magazine article that has their name in it. If an article they write is published, their byline and picture will be larger than the headline.

They will then proceed to send a copy of the article to everyone they know.

Because of their desire for fame, they are easily swayed by the media or celebrity endorsement. They trust big names and equate fame with importance.

So if a pop singer endorses a new programming language, it must be good because the pop singer said so.

If a celebrity endorser goes on tour, this group would volunteer to make the arrangements, carry the luggage, and personally escort the celebrity endorser from city to city. And, because of their attention to detail, everything would go just fine.

You can observe distributors who have this value high on their list. You will see them getting their picture with top leaders and the company president.

And dinner with the president of your company? Oh my! These distributors would crawl over broken glass to qualify for that privilege. Forget the bonuses. Think of how much fun it would be telling stories about the time they had dinner with the president.

Arrange dinners with successful upline leaders. Have these individuals be the masters of ceremonies and do introductions with famous people. (Yes, they will then say, "When the president shared the stage with ME ...")

They love their image. Help them enjoy their image more.

Another value?

Value #12: Popularity.

Stacy is a personal assistant for an advertising executive. At work, she volunteers to assist others and run extra errands. She knows the names of every person in the office and makes uplifting personal comments to them in the morning. Every week she brings flowers and homemade cookies to the office.

Although she is well-liked, she has been passed over for many promotions. Her work is fine, but she doesn't have the time and energy to go that extra mile to qualify for a promotion.

Why? Because she is too busy helping others.

Stacy's social calendar is full. However, she often makes too many commitments and she becomes stressed trying to please everyone. Everyone loves Stacy. That is great because that is what Stacy wants - to be loved.

It is easy to spot people who place a high value on popularity. They have the most friends on every social networking site. They were popular in high school and now want everyone to be their friend. The popular person will frequently agree to anything in order to please someone.

You want the perfect "Yes person"? Here they are.

Sometimes when these people say "Yes," they will have a hard time following through. Why? Because they have already made too many commitments to help others.

Popularity-minded people are great confidence-builders and are able to motivate those around them. People and prospects are naturally attracted to this group of people.

Remember, people in this group make their decisions based not on what is best for them, but based upon how other people will think of them.

Yes, their primary motivation is to make sure other people think of them fondly. This value makes them some of the most helpful and supportive leaders in our group.

Show appreciation to these distributors. Recognize them in front of others and acknowledge their contributions. A standing ovation ... now, that could be the ultimate reward.

Time for another value.

Value #13: Accomplishments.

Martha leaves the house with her "To Do" list clipped prominently on the outside of her leather-bound organizer. She also has a duplicate copy of the "To Do" list for the sun visor in her car.

Every task on the list is assigned a certain number of minutes and Martha knows she can increase her productivity by taking a shortcut down Ninth Street. These lists are important to Martha because she has to balance her time carefully between the Boy Scouts, PTA, Community Center, and the local political party.

There are no unfinished projects on her hobby list.

The person who values her accomplishments compulsively writes out lists so that she can cross things off and feel productive. Her home is filled with diplomas and trophies. She sets up milestones in her life and likes to refer to them.

A talkative person, she will explain in great detail the course of action she took in achieving her latest goal. She likes to tell stories about conquering things and is easy to find in a social setting.

Look for the animated person telling stories to a crowd - endlessly. (Gee, what would a networking get-together be without at least a few of these people?)

While the rest of humanity believes in setting goals and making wish lists, this group sets goals and actually achieves them. When they make a New Year's resolution, they keep it.

This trait makes them consistent achievers and great networkers.

And no, these people aren't shy. They are the talkers.

Motivation means multi-tasking ... don't bore these distributors with a simplistic task. They are performance machines.

Value #14: Desire to have a good time.

Kenneth has an office job. Technically he has an office - he is just not sure exactly where it is. When he is at work, he is usually on the phone with out-of-town friends or making plans with friends for that evening.

He takes off work early two afternoons a week for his racquetball games and is king of the three-hour lunch. When he tells everyone at the office that he "will be back in a minute," they assume he is gone for the day.

People with this value high on their list are relaxed and easy-going. Work to them is a necessary evil but a great way to meet new people. Obviously they prefer jobs that have lots of flex time and free time.

You will find them having dinner with friends or at sporting events instead of working. They favor conventions, web-surfing, and motivational meetings instead of bookkeeping, building a business, and telephone calls.

As extremely social creatures, they spend time playing tennis and golf, going to the bars and hanging out with friends.

What motivates these people? A travel bonus or going to a company convention where they can meet their friends and have fun. You probably won't see them at the company sessions, because they will be touring the city with their friends.

Open-minded? Yes.

This group finds alternative careers and opportunities exciting since they fit in with their values and lifestyles. And there is no danger that anyone in this group will become a workaholic.

Enough values?

There are many more values. But for now, let's see what we can do with this knowledge about the different values people have.

Here is the test.

These are some of the basic values people have. I am sure you recognize that many of your friends and acquaintances are strongly aligned with certain values.

For instance, I mentioned my friend, Mike. Mike's values are travel and adventure first ... and everything else is a distant second place. So what happens when you talk to Mike about network marketing?

If you describe the financial security and the residual income, Mike will politely turn you down. If you didn't understand Mike's values, you would think,

"How could anybody turn down financial security?"

However, if you were to describe the adventure, travel, and challenge in network marketing, then Mike might grab you by the throat and demand that you give him an application to join immediately.

Why?

Because that is what is important in Mike's life. He makes his decisions based on how they will affect his values of travel and adventure.

As a side note, Mike's stay in the U.S. eventually became boring, so he moved to a remote coastal Spanish village. Of course he moved there with no job or any idea of what he would do, but that didn't matter. It was a new adventure!

And did I mention that Mike didn't know a word of Spanish? But you would expect that.

He is presently climbing mountains, participating in the village's never-ending festivals, and having the adventure of a lifetime.

Travel and adventure equal instant motivation to Mike. When talking to Mike, we have to account for his viewpoint of the world.

Back to other people's values.

Once you have established the values of a prospect, it is easy to show him how network marketing can help him satisfy those values. Some people join to make friends, others join to build a residual income. And yes, some even join for travel and adventure like Mike.

Before you evaluate and establish another person's values, why not practice on yourself first?

Here is a chance to rate your own values in order of importance to you. Once you have arranged your list with your most important values at the top, ask yourself this question:

"Do these top few important values explain why I do the things I do?"

I think you will find that the answer is "Yes."

Now, if you have trouble putting your values in descending order, you can usually tell which values are most important to you by the amount of time you invest in them.

For example, everyone likes to say that "family" is a top value, but they tend to spend more time on their careers. Hmmmm. Maybe that would explain your recent decision to work overtime.

Here is the list of values that I described. Please rank them in order of importance in your life:

Values List.

1. Power.

2. Financial security.

3. Desire to be rich.

4. Desire to look good.

5. Loving relationship with partner.

6. Family.

7. Career fulfillment.

8. Desire to feel needed.

9. Personal enlightenment.

10. Adventure/travel/adrenaline junkie.

11. Aim for fame.

12. Popularity.

13. Accomplishments.

14. Desire to have a good time.

Write down which value is the most important to you.

Then, write down the next most important value, etc.

When you are finished, your most important values will be at the top of your list and your least important values will be at the bottom of your list. This should tell you a lot about yourself and the criteria you use to make decisions.

And finally, notice how these most important values shape the direction of your life.

Want to know your distributors' values?

Have them do this same exercise.

This will help you work with them, understand them, and have more empathy for the decisions they make.

And if they won't write down their values, just observe. Their actions and decisions will tell you their values.

Can values change?

Of course, but not right away.

Want to know your prospects' values?

Again, have them do the same exercise.

People make decisions based upon their current values. That is our starting point to understand their present internal motivation.

And finally, want to motivate people?

Easy. Just talk to them about the top values on their list.

MOTIVATION MAY NOT BE THE PROBLEM.

Sometimes people ask, "How do I motivate my downline? They are lazy. They won't make phone calls. They are not bringing anyone to the meetings. They just refuse to contact anyone."

Maybe we are asking the wrong question. Just imagine this scenario:

Our brand-new distributor signs the application. That's it.

Does our new distributor automatically get network marketing skills from signing the application?

No.

So, our untrained distributor goes out and talks to his family and friends. And because he doesn't know "trained words" ... he talks **AT** people. He fails to get his message past the negativity, the skepticism, and the fear of salesmen that his prospects have. The words he chose to say ... did not work.

Now, our new distributor is not stupid. He can see that the words he is saying do not get results. However, he doesn't have any new words to say. Why?

Because we did not teach him how to talk **WITH** people in our training. Our new distributor only knows one-way communication, and that turns prospects off.

After rejection after rejection after rejection, our new distributor feels bad. Our distributor has common sense. He learns that the only way to stop the rejection and pain is to stop talking to people. And then our distributor becomes inactive.

Our new distributor remains motivated. He doesn't have a motivation problem. Instead, he has a **training** problem. No one taught him how to talk with prospects ... correctly.

Who is at fault here?

We are, of course.

So, before we blame his lack of activity on a motivation problem, let's check this first. Did we give our new distributor the skilled word sequences to do the job?

Teach our team.

By learning the basic skills of how to talk to people **correctly**, our new distributor can get positive results. It is easy to be motivated when prospects buy and join.

Some "motivation problems" can be solved by learning basic network marketing skills such as:

- Prospecting.
- Building rapport.
- Ice breakers.
- Presentation skills.
- Story skills, and more.

Instead of encouraging our new distributor to go out and get more rejection, maybe we could invest our time into teaching the new distributor how to talk to people ... correctly.

WATCH PROSPECTS STEAL DEFEAT FROM THE JAWS OF VICTORY.

Sometimes we just have to let go.

Is there a time when we should stop motivating people against their will?

Does this sound familiar?

Before you start your presentation, your prospect objects, "It's a pyramid. I don't want to be involved with that type of business."

After describing how your opportunity is not a pyramid, you begin to show how your business can change your prospect's financial life. However, your prospect has another defense up his sleeve. He shows no interest or enthusiasm for your business. This will give him an easy exit to avoid any success in his life.

But you are good, really good. You finally convince your prospect to be enthusiastic, but then he says,

"Oh, I could never learn to do that business. I am not a salesman. I am not a public speaker. I am not very social. I am not an etc., etc., etc."

Gasp! No matter how much you help your prospect, he still resists his chance for success. So you take 15 minutes to convince him that he can learn the skills to do your business successfully.

Still your prospect continues to find new ways to snatch defeat from the jaws of victory. He says,

"But I just wouldn't be comfortable passing out catalogs at weddings and funerals. I am not comfortable harassing my relatives at Christmas dinner by putting a flipchart over the turkey. I don't want to bother my friends and neighbors, and I don't know anyone else. I just don't think I can do it."

At some point, we finally "get it."

Our prospect is striving for defeat no matter how many chances we give him for victory. Let's accept our prospect's decision and get on with our lives.

Our message of motivation can find more fertile ground with prospects and distributors who want to move forward.

And so the final message is this.

We don't have to motivate everyone. Some people are just self-sabotaging, or stuck where they are. Maybe their dream-sucking vampire employer has already crushed their spirit. They are just waiting to die.

Why not work with people who have just a little bit of momentum already, going forward in their lives? Yes, it is hard to steer a parked car. There has to be some movement forward.

All the motivation examples in this book work better when the person is fertile ground for growth.

THANK YOU.

Thank you for purchasing and reading this book on some of the motivational techniques used in network marketing. I hope you found some ideas that will work for you.

Before you go, would it be okay if I asked a small favor? Would you take just one minute and leave a short review of this book online? Your review can help others choose what they will read next. It would be greatly appreciated by many fellow readers.

I travel the world 240+ days each year.
Let me know if you want me to stop in your
area and conduct a live Big Al training.
BigAlSeminars.com

More Big Al books available at:
BigAlBooks.com

Get the FREE weekly Big Al Report
plus extra bonuses! Sign up today at:
BigAlReport.com

MORE BIG AL BOOKS

The Four Color Personalities for MLM
The Secret Language for Network Marketers

Ice Breakers!
How To Get Any Prospect To Beg You For A Presentation

How To Get Instant Trust, Belief, Influence and Rapport!
13 Ways To Create Open Minds By Talking To The Subconscious Mind

First Sentences for Network Marketing
How To Quickly Get Prospects On Your Side

Big Al's MLM Sponsoring Magic
How to Build a Network Marketing Team Quickly

**How To Prospect, Sell And Build Your
Network Marketing Business With Stories**

**26 Instant Marketing Ideas
To Build Your Network Marketing Business**

How To Build Network Marketing Leaders - Volume One
Step-By-Step Creation Of MLM Professionals

How To Build Network Marketing Leaders - Volume Two
Activities And Lessons For MLM Leaders

Start SuperNetworking!
5 Simple Steps To Creating Your Own Personal Networking Group

How to Follow Up With Your Network Marketing Prospects
Turn Not Now Into Right Now!

Complete list at BigAlBooks.com

ABOUT THE AUTHORS

Keith Schreiter has 20+ years of experience in network marketing and MLM. He is the co-author of the books,

- *51 Ways and Places to Sponsor New Distributors: Discover Hot Prospect For Your Network Marketing Business*

- *How to Follow Up With Your Network Marketing Prospects: Turn Not Now Into Right Now*

- *Start SuperNetworking! 5 Simple Steps To Creating Your Own Personal Networking Group*

Keith shows network marketers how to use simple systems to build a stable and growing business.

So, do you need more prospects? Do you need your prospects to commit instead of stalling? Want to know how to engage and keep your group active? If these are the types of skills you would like to master, you will enjoy his "how-to" style.

Keith speaks and trains in the United States, Canada, and Europe.

Tom "Big Al" Schreiter has 40+ years of experience in network marketing and MLM. As the author of the original "Big Al" training books in the late '70s, he has continued to speak in over 80 countries on using the exact words and phrases to get prospects to open up their minds and say "YES."

His passion is marketing ideas, marketing campaigns, and how to speak to the subconscious mind in simplified, practical ways. He is always looking for case studies of incredible marketing campaigns that give usable lessons.

As the author of numerous audio trainings, Tom is a favorite speaker at company conventions and regional events.

73262782R00098

Made in the USA
San Bernardino, CA
04 April 2018